# HOLIDAYS
## *and* HOLY NIGHTS

# HOLIDAYS
# *and* HOLY NIGHTS

## CELEBRATING TWELVE SEASONAL FESTIVALS
## OF THE CHRISTIAN YEAR

# CHRISTOPHER HILL

Quest Books
Theosophical Publishing House

Wheaton, Illinois ♦ Chennai (Madras), India

The Theosophical Society acknowledges with gratitude
the generous support of the Kern Foundation for the publication of this book.

First Quest Edition 2003

The Theosophical Publishing House
P. O. Box 270
Wheaton, IL 60189-0270

A publication of the Theosophical Publishing House,
a department of the Theosophical Society in America

Cover and text design and typesetting by Beth Hansen-Winter

**Library of Congress Cataloging-in-Publication Data**

Hill, Christopher.
Holidays and holy nights: celebrating twelve seasonal festivals of the Christian
year / Christopher Hill.
    p.   cm.
Includes index.
ISBN 0-8356-0810-7
1. Fasts and feasts—History.   2. Holidays.   3. Church year.   I. Title.

BV43.H55 2003
263'.9—dc21                                         2003046503

5   4   3   2   1   ∗   03   04   05   06   07   08

Printed in Hong Kong through Global Interprint, Santa Rosa, California

This book is dedicated to my mother,
Marjorie Hill.

*"And it was always said of her that she knew how to keep Christmas well,
if anyone alive possessed the knowledge."*

# ❧ ACKNOWLEDGMENTS ❧

Thanks . . .

To Boo, for not giving up, and for all the dinners when Daddy was in the attic. To Evan and Emma, for all the joy and meaning a person could want.

To Norma Easter, formerly of Lyons Township High School (sorry to hand this in so late, Miss Easter); to David McGee, most decent man in the music press; and to Professor William Brady of Knox College: "Not only did Shakespeare believe this—it's true!"

To Katherine "Kitty" Clarke at the DeKoven Center in Racine, Wisconsin, whose enthusiasm kept this project alive.

To Sharron Dorr and Brenda Rosen at Quest Books, for seeing what I hoped someone would see in the manuscript, and then some, and for practicing what they publish. And to gracious and perspicacious editor Jane Lawrence, who is responsible for the resemblance this bears to a professional work (and for all the em-dashes).

Finally, because of a heavy dependence of my thinking about the ritual year upon a particular person, I do want to acknowledge a debt to Ronald Hutton, professor of history at Bristol University, England. He is the preeminent scholar of calendar customs in the English-speaking world as well as a fine and witty writer. His work displays clarity, fair-mindedness, sensitivity, and humility, traits not always present in scholarly writing. He has brought into the scholarly mainstream a field that has been for decades under a cloud of dubious scholarship, popular misconception, and even academic prejudice. I encourage readers of this book to look into any of his major works on the topic, which include:

*Stations of the Sun: A History of the Ritual Year in Britain,* Oxford University Press, 1997.

*The Pagan Religions of the Ancient British Isles: Their Nature and Legacy,* Blackwell Publishers, 1991.

*The Rise and Fall of Merry England: The Ritual Year 1400–1700,* Oxford University Press, 1996.

*The Triumph of the Moon: A History of Modern Pagan Witchcraft,* Oxford University Press, 2001.

*Nothing is so easy as to teach the truth,*
*because the nature of the thing confirms the doctrine.*

—Thomas Traherne

*Nothing you can know that isn't known,*
*Nothing you can see that isn't shown.*

—John Lennon

# CONTENTS

The Four Seasons

# Introduction

## The Time of Your Life

*The Liturgical Year is the supreme vehicle for transmitting the divine life manifested in Jesus Christ.*

—Father Thomas Keating,
*The Mystery of Christ*

*Once we are made aware of the greatness of events as expressions of God's love, once we see and live their sacramental value, then we are liberated into a greater life; the winds of eternity blow about us, and the infinite skies are our home, and we, too, walk the eternal hills.*

—Gerald Vann, O. P., *The Pain of Christ
and the Sorrows of God*

*"What matters it how far we go?" his scaly friend replied.
"There is another shore, you know, upon the other side.
The further off from England the nearer is to France—
Then turn not pale, beloved snail, but come and join the dance.
Will you, won't you, will you, won't you, will you join the dance?"*

—Lewis Carroll, *Alice's Adventures in
Wonderland*

The point, as Jesus of Nazareth once said, is to have life and have it more abundantly, to live the big, deep, rich, adventurous lives our souls were made for. As St. Paul explained, we are heirs of God, members of the household, and so all creation, seen and unseen, is our ancestral home. No matter what kind of cramped, grimy place we currently occupy, we hold the title to a house with many mansions.

This book is not a scholarly study of the Church Year. It is an introduction, a gazetteer, a collection of interesting tidbits. It's a look through an intriguing old trunk up in the attic of Western civilization, which may, as intriguing old boxes in attics should, contain a secret that could take you on an enormous adventure. Somewhere in that trunk is the old will that names you as an heir.

*Holidays and Holy Nights* is about the poetic, symbolic, natural, folkloric, psychological, and mystical nature of the liturgical year. It is about every kind of meaning, some might say, except the strictly theological. I would say that we're unpacking theology. Theology is that trunk in the attic, and we're going to look at what's inside. To say it another way: somewhere, way back, theology came out of actual experience. We're going to go back to get a sense of what that experience was.

Theology is often misunderstood, even by theologians. Church theology is a reflection upon experience, not a substitute for it. Think of it as a rule book for a game. If you had never played basketball and you read a book of basketball rules, you might easily decide that basketball sounds like no fun. The rule book would describe hard, pointlessly repetitive activity governed by a mass of complex and arbitrary regulations. It would give you no idea what it's like to play basketball or why people like to do it. Fortunately, almost no one reads a rule book before they begin to play basketball or any other game. Rule books distill the experience of a lot of people who've been playing the game for a long time, and so they are useful for coaches and physical education teachers. But anybody can go out on the playground and join a pickup game. This book is pickup theology. We're going to toss the ball around and get a feel for the game.

The key to the spiritual life is finding a balance between taking it seriously and taking it lightly; that is, taking it in the right *spirit*. If I were to say, "I don't see any reason to run back and forth trying to throw a ball through a hoop, and you can't make me do it," I would clearly be taking the rules in the wrong spirit. Seen rightly, the rules are in service to the experience, the fun. If we didn't have fun (that is, get more abundant life) out of playing the game, the rules would be pointless. But to have the particular kind of fun of playing basketball, rules

SNAP THE WHIP, BY WINSLOW HOMER, 1872. THE SACRED TIME OF THE CHRISTIAN YEAR COMBINES FORM AND FREEDOM, LIKE A DANCE OR A GAME.

are essential. You can't have a game or a dance without following rules, patterns, and steps. But if the movements and the steps become the most important thing, you've lost the spirit—and the point.

Some may find this approach frivolous or lighthearted. Well, angels fly because they take themselves lightly, as G. K. Chesterton said. "Where the spirit of Christ is, there is freedom," said Paul. "Love God and love your neighbor," said his Master. Notice the order there: from a right relationship with the Creator springs the joy that goes out to other created beings. The Christian year is a way to put our hearts into that right relationship. The Year of the Lord shows our hearts, senses, and imaginations what there is to love about God. If we don't know how to dance, how can we invite others to join in?

Time is a thing that most of us take very seriously. On the other hand, to see the year as a pattern implies something like a game—a children's game, even. The concentric circles of sacred time in the Year of the Lord—the seasons, days, and hours—direct us step-by-step to this present moment in which we exist, this "moment of Christ," which is always a holiday.

T. S. Eliot wrote that "without the still point, there would be no dance, and there is only the dance." Learning to balance on the still point is like that strange, gravity-defying act called riding a bicycle, that act of learning to depend on something unknown to your thinking mind. It's hard; it seems to go against your nature at first. And yet there you go.

## Patterns and Rhythms

We in the West are oriented to the future. We strive to be ever new, to regenerate the world. Our civilization has accomplished a lot this way. But we've lost something, too. We have gone along with a flow of events that has somehow ended up making us too busy to respond to that buried sense of the heart that says there must be more: more meaning, more color, deeper excitement. We live in a world where so many authoritative voices—the successful, the influential, even the scholarly—say that commerce and power are all there is; a world where we work fifty-hour weeks for years, then get five days off. We are all Bob Cratchits these days, chained in our money-changing cubbyholes for hours that even Ebenezer Scrooge would hesitate to demand.

Charles Dickens saw a world around him in which technological and commercial progress was threatening to throw something in human nature out of whack forever. Technological and commercial man was gaining the world in the nineteenth century but losing the cosmos—the connection to the great patterns of life. At that time, Christmas and the whole ritual calendar of traditional Britain were fast vanishing. No "Charles Dickens Christmas" existed when Charles Dickens wrote *A Christmas Carol*, just a few fading rags of old customs. A Charles Dickens Christmas is what Charles Dickens created. Dickens's resurrection of Christmas was a response to the crisis created by the Industrial Revolution, and it was a major victory in the struggle to keep humanity human.

Many people today want the extra dimension to life that a festive ritual cycle offers. Festivals are a sign that humanity is more real than the realism of the market, that we are all citizens of a great and mysterious realm. The poet William Blake (also during the time of the Industrial Revolution) wrote about the "mind-forg'd manacles" that we wear. He meant the shutting down of our awareness of our true stature and the big life that is our birthright. He saw these manacles in the subordination of human beings to materialism and productivity. The ritual year of the Church is one way out of the manacles. Time—the very device by which we measure productivity and results—is the key.

# *A Personal Note*

While we're on the subject of Christmas . . .

This book exists mainly because I never got over Christmas. As for a lot of us, that's when I first experienced a time that carried a special charge and stood apart from the rest of time—time that had something enormous looming behind it. I was not satisfied with Christmas being a once-a-year experience. It was clearly what life was supposed to be like all the time.

I found some common threads between Christmas and other times in my life. Some of them were other holidays. Halloween—indeed, the whole month of October—offered a less intense version. Vacations had a little of it. So did Easter, although this was mostly because Eastertime was when they showed old biblical epics on TV, and so the drama of Holy Week was linked for me with the lure of ancient and exotic lands. But we were not churchgoers in my family, and the rest of the Christian holy days meant nothing to me.

As an adolescent in the midsixties, I began to catch wind of things happening in London and San Francisco. People who were interested in a more festive life, one that seemed to take into account these things I had glimpsed, a life that incorporated mystery and was not lived in ordinary time, caught my attention. Eventually, certain authors and teachers—especially C. S. Lewis and Father Paul Blighton, founder of a Christian contemplative order in San Francisco in the midsixties—began to suggest to me that what I was looking for was in some way connected with Christianity, a truly off-the-wall notion for me at that point. But I followed it up. In a way, I came back around to Christmas.

As I got to know the Church, what resonated most for me was the liturgical year. Here was something clearly related to my childhood experiences. But at that time (the early seventies) the Church did not see the liturgical year as a great selling point. I suppose it seemed an old, churchy, fussy, complicated concept—not relevant to the social and political concerns of a Baby Boom generation that the Church was anxious to attract. To me, on the contrary, it seemed that this vision of the sacred in the turning year would have appealed powerfully to the spiritual longing at the root of the counterculture.

Today we Baby Boomers are middle-aged, with several minigenerations in our wake, and the Church is still struggling with a way to offer itself to all of us. But I think there is a growing sense that the future of the Church lies with all those people who want ritual, sacred experience, transformation, and a way to live in harmony with the large patterns and rhythms of existence. I believe that sacred time is the great gift that the liturgically based communions have to offer spiritual seekers today.

## Sacred Time

In this book I'm interested in the *experience* of sacred time, in our ability to feel the intersection of time and eternity at special places in the year. As I've said, many of us know what sacred time is like from our experience of Christmas, especially as children. I strongly believe that this experience does not have to be—in fact, shouldn't be—limited to Christmas or to childhood. It is the heritage of all humans. It is one of those treasures that the Church can and should take out of the trunk and offer to everyone. Sacred time is what makes the Church Year a genuinely transformative spiritual practice. But except for people deeply invested in the liturgical life, such as monastics and some clergy, our experience of sacred time is limited.

Three things must come together to open up the experience of sacred time: the ritual and theology of the Church, cultural and/or family tradition, and the natural cycles and environment.

In addition to these basics, there's another ingredient without which the magic won't work. We need to feel imaginatively free with the festivals. We need to make them our own and blend them with the stuff of our lives and the world around us—to play with them. This freedom is part of the glorious liberty of the children of God that Paul talked about. Most of us are so comfortable with Christmas that we easily weave its sacred atmosphere into loves and friendships, family relationships, activities, little rituals, music we listen to, walks we take, memories we cherish, treasured objects and possessions, things we eat and drink. We feel free to invent things about Christmas. In our hearts and imaginations we have a pretty good grasp of what Christmas means and have no problem applying it to enhance our lives. Christmas as an idea gives meaning to the time of year, to the cycles of our lives, to the natural and human world around us. And these things give meaning to Christmas—back and forth, in mutually enriching rhythm.

One of the points of this book is that we do know some of the other festivals in our hearts more than we think we do. We just don't always know the theological name for what we feel. My hope is that this book will help evoke that knowledge, help you recognize the festivals in your hearts so that you'll turn to the liturgy and think, How amazing that the Church knows and celebrates this!

# *Time*

The whole point of the Year of the Lord is that there is more than one way to experience time. The understanding of time that most people live with is only one way to experience it. We could call it the worldly or profane understanding of time. It is an image of time as a straight horizontal line with a middle point, where we stand, called the Present. This line is always moving past us like a conveyor belt. On the left is the Past, where present moments constantly flow and immediately cease to exist. On the right is the Future, which is always moving toward the Present, but never actually arrives.

This model is almost completely abstract. In other words, we never actually experience any of it. The present is gone before we're aware of it, and the Past and Future lie outside our grasp. Anxiety is built into it. Each human possesses only a limited quantity of this kind of time, and it is constantly passing us by, never to return.

This view of time is not necessarily bad. It can be a useful tool. All human progress, in a sense, depends on it. But it's not the whole or most important part of the picture. It is not the way we experience time in the deepest parts of ourselves, on the level of our hearts, and it is not the way God experiences time. Above and below this abstract, one-dimensional timeline is, well, reality. This is the world we actually experience, in which we "live and move and have our being," as Paul said. The world of "I Am," as God introduced himself to Moses. The present moment is eternity.

For most of human history, people experienced time very differently. The pattern was not a line but a circle or cycle. The cycles of sun, moon, and stars; of the seasons; of the life, death, and birth of plants, animals, and human beings. Everything went away, but then in some way everything always came back. We can be sure that people living with this image of time still got anxious about things, but anxiety wasn't built into the system itself.

The image of the cycle contains a lot of truth. It expands the one-dimensional timeline into a two-dimensional circle and so takes in a lot more of reality. It is less abstract than the line, truer to experience, and incorporates the fundamental patterns of creation. Years, seasons, months, weeks, days, and hours all come from this model of time. Birth, life, death, and rebirth are all in it. What it doesn't include is the possibility of growth. In the cycle, the more things change, the more they stay the same.

The Year of the Lord, the Christian understanding of time, is a variation on the cycle. The timeline, as we've said, is a one-dimensional model. The circle is two-dimensional. The

Year of the Lord is three-dimensional: It is modeled on the spiral, a circle that grows outward and upward. It grows in a vertical direction as well as horizontally, combining the straight line of past, present, and future with the height and depth of eternity. Like a spiraling tornado, it sucks one-dimensional time up into three-dimensional reality. It uses time to break us out of time. It hallows or sacralizes time and transforms it into eternity. Year, season, month, week, day and hour, all make concentric circles that lead deeper and deeper into the center, the present moment, where we live in the presence of God. The present is the Presence. And then present time ripples outward again, connecting us with all time and all the cosmos.

Here's an example. In the Christian image of time, Christ's Incarnation is the turning point of history. Its counterpart in the year, one ring further in, is Christmas. Christmas comes at the time of the winter solstice, the darkest day and turning point of the year. In the next ring—the day—Christmas is analogous to midnight, the darkest hour of night and the turning point toward dawn. The Christian day is divided into eight "Hours" (each three hours long). Each Hour has its own "Office" or worship service. The Hours are analogous to the seasons. The first two Hours after midnight, Matins and Prime—from midnight to 6:00 A.M.—are analogous to winter.

If we open our imaginations to reflect on Christ coming into history, eternity coming into time, it will tell us something about what happens every Christmas. If we reflect on the feeling and meaning of Christmas, it will tell us something about the middle of the night. If we reflect on the middle of the night, it will reveal something about the dark hours of our lives and teach us something about how our souls work. Knowing more about our souls teaches us more about the life of Christ. The life of Christ teaches us about how divine life works. In and out, cosmic to intimate, great to small, macro to micro, and back again, the year of the Lord connects us to God as the spokes of a bicycle wheel connect hub to rim. Each year, season, day, moment, reenacts the great story that takes place in our souls and in the life of God. Each instant that we are conscious, Christ is born in us; each present instant is Christmas. At each instant, we die to time and awake in eternity. Each present instant is Easter.

To the degree that you can see time as a pattern, you are beginning to see from outside time. The Christian year makes us less and less prisoners of straight-line time. Like all things that are done by rhythm, like playing a game or dancing, time becomes an activity joined freely, not dictated by need or fear. The anxiety built into straight-line time is gradually transformed into joy. Tuning our life to that rhythm helps us, year by year, live more in the eternal present and less in T. S. Eliot's "ridiculous . . . waste, sad time, before and after." To use an image from Judeo-Christian mythology, as soon as man and woman stepped out of the garden, the meter started to run. The liturgical year is a way back into the garden.

## God and the Solar System

*Christ has given a special meaning and power to the cycle of the seasons, which of themselves are good and by their very nature have a capacity to signify our life in God. Jesus has made this ebb and flow of light and darkness, activity and rest, birth and death, the sign of a higher life, a life [which] we live in Him.*

—Thomas Merton,
*Seasons of Celebration*

*His invisible attributes, that is to say his everlasting power and deity, have been visible, ever since the world began, to the eye of reason, in the things he has made.*

—St. Paul,
Letter to the Romans 1:19

*Sun and moon perform their stately dance for the salvation of the world.*

—Bishop Origen of Alexandria

Christianity is a sacramental religion, but it doesn't always act like it. *The Book of Common Prayer* defines sacrament as "an outward and visible sign of inward and spiritual grace." In other words, the created world, nature, and our senses reflect and bring the Divine to us. This understanding of the created world is why Jesus thought that ordinary, real bread and wine can help bring us into the life of God. But this truth is not limited to the few rites of the Church that are technically labeled sacraments, any more than the effect of Christ in the world is limited to the short life of Jesus of Nazareth.

It's good to remember that God came before Christianity. He came before Judaism, before religion, before humanity. He came before the world, the solar system, and the universe. He made the universe in his image. Everything that God made is, as Paul said, a sacrament of God. The way God is, is reflected in the growth of the grass, the conception of children, the turning of the earth, and its circuit around the sun.

Most (if not all) early human cultures had a sacramental view of the natural cycles. Now, it's true that there is not much talk in the New Testament about festivals and the rhythms of nature (although, of course, the Passion happens at the time of the supreme Jewish festival of Passover). But partly that's because people took the cycle of festivals completely for granted. No one imagined a year without them. The life of the Jewish people was built on a rich structure of festivals that had their roots in the agricultural and nomadic history of the peoples of that land. Scholars have seen that many of the major events in the life of Jesus, especially in the Gospel of John, reflect the cycle of these festivals.

Since the first Christians were Jews, much of the Christian calendar is based on Jewish practice. In the first centuries of the Christian Era, the fathers and mothers of the Church used the existing Jewish festival calendar as their foundation as they created new customs and liturgy. It came very naturally to them to imagine the work of Christ acted out in the rhythm of the year.

The working of nature and the universe is a very deep sacrament of God. This is not a Christian truth or a pagan truth, a Muslim truth or a Hindu truth. It's just a truth. In certain eras, some Christians have talked as if the seasonal rites of the Church were a lingering stain left over from benighted pagan nature worship, from fertility cults with their presumably depraved rites. While it's true that certain cultures in certain periods observed the seasons with horrible practices, that is not the fault of the solar system nor of God. Humans are clearly capable of abusing any part of creation. From time to time in Church history, voices have cried out against "nature worship" and "paganism" and "popery" when they thought people were paying too much attention to the sacramental power of the seasons. Our problem today is the opposite. Instead of paying too much attention to this face of God (if that's possible), we pay far too little.

## *The Greatest Story Ever Told*

In the early stages of writing this book, I thought about calling it *The Drama of the Christian Year*. What I mean by *drama* is pretty much the dictionary definition: "a succession of events with the dramatic progression or emotional content typical of a play." The Year of the Lord is a succession of events with a dramatic progression; in other words, a story. This dramatic quality is the most appealing thing about the Christian year.

It is a deep and old human instinct to sense a story in the year, to feel a huge but hard-to-express significance in the progression of the sun and the turning of the seasons. When early humans began to express this feeling, they naturally turned it into stories. There were stories about darkness battling against light; stories of kings, heroes, and gods rising to the height of glory and power, only to go down into darkness again. And sometimes, in some way, to return.

Mythologies, religions, and rituals were born from these stories. In a sense, *all* stories were born from this first and simplest of stories. Birth, adventure, triumph, conflict, death, return—the pattern underlies human narrative from the oldest folktales to the daily newspaper. This pattern is the DNA of our imaginations—a code at the base of all our thinking that we express over and over in thousands of different ways. It's almost as if we can't open our mouths to speak without our words taking this shape.

Most of the traditions that expressed the meaning of the year—parish life, local customs, even the rituals of professional life—have disappeared, or their social influence has faded. But our DNA hasn't changed. The dim sense of meaning is still there, even when the customs and traditions have gone. Spring, fall, summer, and winter are still telling us something we can't quite grasp, like music heard in another room. In a way, we're back to square one. As did our earliest ancestors, we feel the vague but huge significance and look for a way to say something about it, to be a part of it. We cling to this yearning in sweet, silly observances— Labor Day picnics, opening day at the ball park, trick-or-treating, Thanksgiving turkeys, Christmas pageants, summer vacations.

The Year of the Lord helps us hear the story the year is telling us. It is the latest version in history of that story. It is a very complete, rich, and sophisticated working out of the spiritual implications of the year story. The enormous being whose story the year tells is God. The drama that the year acts out—of birth, adventure, triumph, conflict, death, and resurrection—is the drama of God. This is how God lives and works in his own eternal nature, in physical nature, and in human nature in our souls.

Of course, as a force that shapes societies, the Christian year too has faded over the last centuries. But that doesn't mean that it isn't still there for anyone who wants it. The Year of the Lord is a living tradition. Its rites have been celebrated without a break for millennia; its roots stretch back even further, into prehistory. It has a full body of writing, thinking, and understanding that supports and expands on it. And somewhere, not very far from you, this very week, a group of people is keeping these ancient traditions alive. This is happening in a church, of course, particularly one that emphasizes its liturgy—Roman Catholic, Anglican/ Episcopalian, Eastern Orthodox, and, to a degree, Lutheran.

# *Paganism*

*Now, the phenomenon, admitted on all hands, is this, that the great portion of what is generally received as Christian truth . . . is to be found in heathen philosophies and religions. . . . We think that scripture bears us out in saying that the Moral Governor of the world has scattered the seeds of truth far and wide over its extent; that these have variously taken root and grown up as in the wilderness, wild plants indeed, but living. . . . We even hold that one special way in which providence has imparted divine knowledge to us has been by enabling [the Church] to draw and collect it together out of the world.*

—John Cardinal Newman

Today, many people who want to find meaning in the year are attracted to what is loosely called *paganism*. Modern paganism might seem like a New Age, postsixties phenomenon. But it has been gathering steam for a while now—at least since the late nineteenth century. Its participants often describe it as a revival of the pre-Christian religions of Europe.

It attracts me, too. To find a sense of the great mystery in seasonal rites—in the wisdom and lore of the preindustrial world, in the mysteries of plants and animals, in a sense of connectedness to our ancestors—is natural, human, and good. Folklore, myths, legends, gods and goddesses, traditions and customs point us to real wisdom. Paganism in this sense doesn't imply any particular pre-Christian religion. It's another name for the world of the unconscious mind—the source of imagination, vision, art, poetry, dreams. The Year of the Lord gets its raw material from here. The Church desperately needs more input from this source.

The sacred places, rites, and calendars of humanity all seem to have one thing in common. They are ways to bring the patterns of creation and the divine creative power into our lives, to make our lives on earth reflect or repeat the way things are above or before time: "Your will be done on earth as it is in heaven," and "As it was in the beginning, it is now and ever shall be." The Year of the Lord continues the primordial human project of relating oneself to a cosmic movement.

But I believe that the Church Year also brings something new to the party. Despite the horror and misery of history right up to this present moment, I do believe that humanity is evolving spiritually. For this reason, our rites need to become more human and more profound to accommodate our developing consciousness.

As a new version of the ancient human calendar, the Year of the Lord reflects how humanity has changed over the ages. It deepens the celebration in a number of ways. It takes us deeper than nature, reaching through nature into the divine life for which nature itself is a symbol. It has more to do with human individuality. It is kinder. It pays more attention to what is happening within us. Instead of watching the sun in the sky and sensing "through a glass darkly" that this has something to do with us, as prehistoric people did, the Christian calendar looks at both the sun in the sky and the sun/Son within us. In attempting to reflect something even bigger than nature, it becomes, paradoxically, about something as individual and intimate as each of our lives, our seasons and days. It is more democratic. The rites are no longer for the land, the crops, the herds, the tribe, the king, the sun, but for us—each and every one of us. In addition to being witnesses or subjects of cosmic events, we are participants. Our risings, settings, and resurrections are as important as the sun's—more important, actually. It is more hopeful that, unlike the sun and grass, we not only return but are resurrected, revealing a new potential with each cycle.

There's great power and fascination in old seasonal rites and traditions. When we read or hear about them, they have a strange, evocative quality; they feel almost like memories. Modern neopagans would say that this feeling is our intuitive response to the Old Religion of prehistoric Europe, to the pagan traditions that were given a Christian coating over the centuries.

I don't think that's exactly the case. Western Christian culture has, at this point, been around for an almost Egyptian span of time. Over these many centuries, the common people of Europe created a kind of folk-Christianity, weaving in much from the time before Europe became Christian. But this was not, as neopagans believe, the Old Religion disguised as Christian celebration. Christian and pre-Christian traditions became a real synthesis, a distinct religious culture. To get a feel for what this old unity was like, look in the *Carmina Gaedelica*, an anthology of prayers, hymns, incantations, and blessings from Gaelic-speaking farmers and fishermen in Scotland, collected by Alexander Carmichael in the late nineteenth century. Out of things that are clearly Christian *and* clearly pre-Christian, these people created a new thing with its own beautiful, strange, and unmistakable atmosphere. If you tried peeling back the Christian layers, you would, in reality, be tearing half of it away. As G. K. Chesterton said, paganism is simply the story of humanity. Christianity does not stand apart from and sealed off from this story, as both its friends and enemies have sometimes claimed.

The Christian year, experienced in all its richness, incorporates paganism. Christian wisdom absorbs the wisdom of humanity before it—how could it not? The broad historical tendency of mainstream orthodox Christianity (with, admittedly, some major exceptions) has not been to winnow out paganism, but to baptize, regenerate, and integrate all that is truly human.

## The Structure of This Book

The purpose of this book is to help give the Christian year back to the "mind of the faithful"—to reappropriate the Christian seasons and festivals for the enriched imagination of everyone.

I've chosen twelve feasts or seasons of the Christian year. The selection is not scholarly, methodical, or even representative. I've chosen some because they're important, some because they're obscure, and some just because they strike my fancy. I've tried to spread my choices fairly evenly through the year. In general, the descriptions of the feasts and seasons follows the liturgy of the Anglican (including the Episcopal) Church as found in *The Book of Common Prayer* and *Lesser Feasts and Fasts* (except for St. Brigid of Ireland, whom I gratefully borrow from the Roman Catholics). The information and comments apply to Roman Catholic tradition as well, except where noted. The Eastern Orthodox Church is a different kettle of fish. Its calendar, liturgy, and theology are sometimes quite distinct from those of Western churches, though I have used insights and examples from that amazing body of wisdom to enrich this book.

Each entry has three parts. The first is a meditation on the feast, fast, or season, called "The Experience." This part is intended to do a number of things:

- trigger the sense of recognition discussed above—that you do already, in some way, know the festivals in your hearts;
- suggest ways that the themes, images, and rites can be unfolded, savored, reflected on, lived with; to explore the light they shed on life outside "Church"; to be an example of the kind of imaginative freedom we have with the liturgy;
- illustrate how the liturgy and the rhythms of nature work an alchemy together, giving depth and meaning to each other;
- suggest how full imaginative participation in the Year of the Lord can create the experience of sacred time at many different points in the year.

There follows a section called "The Story" that gives informational background on the feast: its historic origins and how it developed over time. It gives a sketch of the holiday's theological meaning, how it fits in with the whole faith and the rest of the Church Year, and how the festival is observed in folk customs—examples of the ways that people have imaginatively responded to the feasts, developing the meaning of the holiday with elements from their native cultures.

In the third part, called "Entering the Season," I offer some suggestions for ways that you can personally respond to the holy times and incorporate the meaning of the liturgy into the rest of life. Some of the ideas are things that my own family does or has done. Others come from the numerous fine writers who have written books specifically about seasonal and religious family activities. Some are folk customs that you can recreate.

The book begins with a chapter on the history and structure of the Church Year—how it developed and how it works. It's a basic introduction to how the Christian tradition has designed time, a sort of schematic diagram of this machine for turning time into eternity.

## *Godspeed*

There is much in life that makes us feel small, that takes our stature and dignity from us. The World (in the theological sense, the socially and economically constructed world) is an extremely powerful device for narrowing and distracting our awareness of life. The World wields powerful, subtle, time-tested ploys for fragmenting our attention toward a million objects, through desire, fear, anxiety, social pressure, the whole vast sophisticated bag of tricks that the media and the economy lay out in front of us. William Wordsworth understood: "The world is too much with us, early and late, getting and spending, we lay waste our powers." Like Esau in the Bible, we sell our birthright for a bowl of soup. Like the Prodigal Son, we squander our inheritance. "In headaches and in worry, vaguely life leaks away," as W. H. Auden knew.

The Year of the Lord is a wheel that rolls in the opposite direction, back up the path toward home. It helps us collect ourselves, gather ourselves back up instead of losing ourselves in a thousand different meaningless places. It helps us to lead lives a little truer to our yearning for Something Else. To live entirely on the timeline is to be a slave; to step onto the spiral of sacred time is to begin the slow journey to freedom, to the wide sublime highlands we were made for.

Let's take the map out of the trunk and go.

ST. CATHERINE'S MONASTERY, SINAI. *THE CHRISTIAN PATTERN OF TIME DEVELOPED IN EARLY MONASTIC SETTLEMENTS.*

# 1

# THE ORIGINS OF
# THE CHRISTIAN YEAR

Like the yeast in Jesus' parable of the housewife's bread, the Christian calendar started small and grew until it filled the year. At the very beginning, in the first months or years after Jesus' death, the basic observance for Jesus' followers was probably daily prayer. In that era, devout Jews observed regular times of prayer throughout the day, a reminder that time was subject to and originated in eternity. This prayer usually involved recitations of the Psalms, Israel's great poetic narrative of the soul's intimate, tempestuous relationship with God. In group worship, the Psalms were probably sung or chanted; the chant of the Christian Church originated in this Jewish contemplative practice.

The first Christian monastics, in the deserts of Egypt and Sinai, adapted this cycle of recitations and made it the structure of their day. The practice consecrated the daily round hour by hour. The hourly recitations became the basic pattern of Christian life. Christian chant, eventually collected under Pope Gregory and thus called Gregorian chant, is intended to deepen the contemplative experience of observing the cycles of day and night. Known in the Church as the Liturgy of the Hours or the Divine Office, this prayer is the basic daily spiritual work of the Church. In orthodox theory, all churches and all ordained persons are obliged to sanctify the cycle of each day by offering some form of the prayer of the hours.

The Christian Hour does not refer to sixty minutes of clock time. The sequence and length of the hours comes from the Roman system of dividing the day into three-hour periods. An hour in the Christian sense is more like a small season within the small year of the day. The Christian day begins with the three night vigils of Matins, from 6 P.M. to 9 P.M., from 9 P.M. to midnight, and from midnight to 3 A.M. Then comes the Hour of Prime, from 3 A.M. to 6 A.M., with the Office of Lauds recited at dawn. The day periods include Terce, from 6 A.M. to 9 A.M.; Sext, from 9 A.M. to noon; and None, from noon to 3 P.M. Evening consists of Vespers, from 3 P.M. to 6 P.M., with Compline recited at 6 P.M.

The Christian day is about responding to the nature of the hour, not working to a schedule. The proper question is not, what time is it? Rather, we should ask, what is it time *for*—work or leisure, community or solitude, waking or rest, praying, eating, reading? In the holy rhythm of the day, each part of the whole is expressed through one of the Hours. Dividing the day in this way reverses the profane sense of time; the clock becomes a servant of the holy human pattern. In *Liturgy for Living*, Charles Price and Louis Weill write that the Hours remind us that the Christian structure of time resembles a crystal. Crystals of a particular substance can be large or small, but the pattern and proportion remain the same. No matter how large or small the unit of time, the same divine pattern is reflected in it. The Christian day is a small crystal of the year.

# Sunday

Jesus' followers not only observed the Jewish pattern of praying the Psalms through the day, they continued to keep the Jewish calendar. They sanctified the Sabbath and celebrated the Jewish holy days. But very early on, the Christian community added something new—the Lord's Day, the Day of the Sun.

The astrological dedication of the seven weekdays to specific planets, and the first day of the week to the sun, originated in Egypt and was eventually accepted around the Mediterranean world. The Christians said that the Lord had been resurrected on Sunday, the first day of the Jewish week. Each week, the Christians participated in the death and Resurrection of the Lord in the central Christian sacrament of the Eucharist.

This first distinctly Christian holy day was from the start not just a commemoration of a past event but a real reenactment, on the spiritual level, of the resurrection within each individual. This pattern would hold true for the whole Christian ordering of time.

Sunday being a working day, Christian communities would rise before dawn for their celebrations or meet for the Eucharistic meal at the end of the day. It was frequently

First-century Jewish tomb in Jerusalem. *The first Easters may have been celebrated in caves or tombs—wombs of the new sacred time.*

assumed around the Mediterranean world that these early risers were sun worshippers. The whole late-classical world had been moving toward what has been called a "solar monotheism"—the many different cults and traditions focusing on the sun as a central unifying image. The Christian movement, while maintaining the distinct character of Jesus of Nazareth, also entered imaginatively into this process. From early on, the harmony between the image of the resurrected Lord and the rising sun was recognized and developed in the Christian imagination. In sun symbolism, early Christians found a way to express and explore the themes of the Passion and Resurrection. This identification of the Son with the sun was the start of Christianity's creative encounter with the myths of the Mediterranean world.

## Building the Pattern: Easter

The Christian year is built around two cycles of festivals—the Christmas cycle of birth and the Easter cycle of death and resurrection. Of these two, Easter came first.

Indeed, aside from celebrating the Eucharist, Easter was what Christians did; it was their central "cultic act." The Easter Vigil of the new light, the initiation and illumination of candidates by the light of the risen Christ was, from the very beginning, the crucial Christian event. It was where the new relationship with the Divine, the good news, began. The whole Christian system—all Christian practice, community, ritual, and organization—developed as a way to realize the effect of Easter in people's lives. Easter was what made Christianity a religion; without it, the Jesus movement would simply have been the adherents of a charismatic rabbi.

The date of Easter is determined by the date of the Jewish festival of Passover; the Latin name for Easter—*Pascha*—is a translation of *Pesach*, the Hebrew word for Passover. One of the facts about the historical Jesus that is most certain is the date of his death. The crucifixion happened when Jesus and his followers, along with thousands of other Jews, came to Jerusalem for Pesach. Jesus was executed on the Friday before the Passover Sabbath. According to the three synoptic Gospels—Matthew, Mark, and Luke—the Last Supper, on the Thursday night before Jesus' execution, was a Passover meal, or *seder*. The author of the Gospel of John disagrees, but he still sets the Last Supper and Crucifixion at Passover time.

Passover is a spring feast. It celebrates the events of the Exodus from Egypt, especially the night on which the destroying angel passed over the homes of the Hebrew slaves while

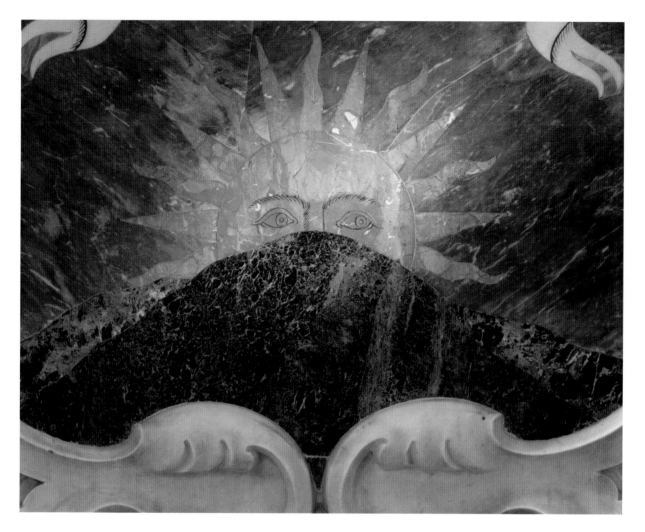

DETAIL OF MOSAIC IN SAN PAOLO MAGGIORE, 1641. *IN THE BEGINNING WAS THE SUN—SYMBOL OF GOD AND THE SOURCE OF TIME, SACRED AND SECULAR.*

killing the firstborn of the Egyptians. The sign for the angel to pass over Hebrew homes was the blood of a sacrificed lamb smeared on the doorposts. In Christian reflection afterward, Jesus took on a symbolic role as the sacrificial victim, taking the place of the Passover or *paschal* lamb.

The Jewish calendar is lunar. The beginning and end of the month are determined by the moon, and a year consists of twelve lunar cycles, not one revolution of the sun. Thus, lunar dates drift in relation to the dates of the solar calendar. Passover falls on the first full moon following the vernal equinox. Easter follows on the first Sunday after that full moon. This way of figuring means that Easter can fall on more than a month of possible days.

There was a long and sometimes bitter controversy in the Church over the dating of Easter. Part of the controversy had to do with whether Easter should have a fixed date, like Christmas, and move through the days of the week (breaking its link to Passover), or whether it should continue to follow the Jewish lunar calendar. The latter view won. To this day in the Western Church, Easter and Passover still move together, with Easter following the first spring full moon.

As a result, the other Christian feasts that depend on Easter for their date (the whole Lent and Easter cycle—Shrove Tuesday, Ash Wednesday, Palm Sunday, and Good Friday—and the events after Easter, like Ascension and Pentecost) are "moveable feasts." They occur on different dates each year depending on the date of Easter. Thus the largest part of the Christ cycle is based on the Jewish calendar. In fact, some of the important days, like Pentecost, are direct Christian adaptations of Jewish feasts.

## *Pentecost*

The second major feast of the early Church, in historical order, was Pentecost, the coming of the Holy Spirit. *Pentecost* is Greek for "fifty days"—fifty days after Passover. It's the Greek name for the Jewish festival of *Shavuoth*, the festival of the first fruits, when Jews brought an offering from the first grain harvest to the Temple in Jerusalem. As Jewish Christians celebrated Shavuoth, it came to express the new life that was coming to fruition within each of them through the completed work of Christ. At Pesach, the seeds began to grow. At Shavuoth/Pentecost, the first fruits of the new life could be enjoyed.

In the Christian cycle, the fifty days between Easter Sunday and Pentecost became known as the *mystagogy*, the time for teaching the mysteries. This time was patterned on the days between Jesus' Resurrection and Ascension, when the risen Christ was still on earth with his disciples. During this period, he taught them truths that he could not teach until he—and they—had experienced Easter. Thus for the Church, Pentecost was the time for the intensive instruction of those newly initiated at Easter.

The Book of Acts tells a story full of powerful symbols to describe the experience of Pentecost. Jesus' followers are gathered for Shavuoth when they hear the sound of a rushing wind. A tongue of flame, the Holy Spirit, appears over each of their heads. The individual

Jesus has gone into eternity and returned to live within each person as the Holy Spirit. In an ecstasy, Jesus' followers speak in a universal language that the people of all nations can understand. Each one of them now possesses the power—symbolized by the flame—to go out from Jerusalem and spread the story of the new life. At Pentecost it becomes clear that all people can understand the good news.

## The Green Season

The life cycle of Christ in the liturgy is orchestrated to the sun in its rising, from its lowest point at the winter solstice almost to its highest. (In years with a late Easter, Pentecost can fall within two weeks of the summer solstice.)

In the fully developed Church Year, the day of Pentecost is followed by the long season called the "weeks after Pentecost"—about half the year. After the huge drama of the first half of the year, the time between Pentecost and Advent, though full of saints' days and other feasts (some of great theological importance), can seem rather empty. The Church calls it, evocatively, "Ordinary Time," time that is ordinal or measured.

But the Church also calls this period "the green season"—the time of ripening. The color of the liturgical vestments is green. The great work has been accomplished. God and nature are joined, and redeemed creation is fruitful. This period reaches a kind of peak at the August Feast of the Transfiguration, when the Pope crushes ripe grapes into the chalice at St. Peter's and Orthodox priests bless the orchards heavy with fruit. After that, the festivals of Michaelmas and All Hallows sanctify the harvest, the fall, and the rising dark—all in preparation for the new beginning.

## Christmas

It took the Church several centuries to determine how the birth of Jesus worked as part of the spiritual program of the year. Christmas did not become an established festival, celebrated on December 25, until the fourth century.

There were various reasons for the delay in celebrating Christmas. None of Jesus' first followers would have had any problem remembering the date of his death. But Jesus had no followers on the date of his birth, and probably no one knew his exact birthday. The Crucifixion and Resurrection, and a conviction of their significance, were a matter of experience and memory for the first Christians. Jesus' birth and its significance were a matter of conjecture.

The vision of Jesus as the divine Son of God, or God incarnate, grew in reflection upon the Resurrection and its meaning. Next came the question, when? When had Jesus become divine? His earliest followers may have believed that Jesus did not become divine until the Resurrection. Other early Christians believed that Jesus was adopted as God's son—that God incarnated in Jesus—at his baptism by John in the River Jordan. Long before Christmas became a holy day, generations celebrated Jesus' baptism as an important festival day.

Others wondered whether Jesus was divine from the time of his birth or, rather, from his conception. Was that when God united with human nature? If Christ's birth was not the moment when God entered the human world, then observing his birthday would be merely a commemoration, not a spiritual reenactment—a day of remembering, not of participating. The full understanding of the Incarnation—of Christ existing from the beginning with God and entering flesh with his literal conception and birth—was worked out and established as orthodox doctrine over the first centuries of this era. Only after the theological questions were settled could Christmas enter the liturgy and its rituals be instituted.

With Jesus' historical birthday forgotten, the winter solstice was the obvious and appropriate time for the ritual—the newborn sun/Son entering and illuminating the worldly darkness. But unlike Passover, the observance of the solstice had no root in Judaism. This was a second reason for the long wait for Christmas to be established. The solstitial celebration of Christmas was probably not possible until the final break between Church and synagogue.

The primordial drama of the winter solstice had made the time a festival for humans everywhere. The December Saturnalia was one of the great Roman holidays. In the birth of light at the darkest time of year, the early Christians saw not just a symbol but an actual enactment on the natural level of the universal truth of the Incarnation. As we've said, many of the religions of the Empire were moving toward a kind of pagan monotheism centered on the symbol of the sun. In the third century, the Empire adopted the birth of the sun on December 25 (at that time, winter solstice fell a bit later than it does today) as an official holiday. Some of the classical world mystery religions even spoke of the advent of the new year as "the virgin giving birth."

When the Easter and Christmas cycles were in place, the structure of the new ritual year was essentially complete. Through Jesus Christ, God comes down into human nature at the darkest time of year. The divine victim is sacrificed, buried, and resurrected, carrying human nature fully into the life of God at seedtime, as spring is fully established on earth. A period of spiritual preparation for Easter was gradually formalized into Lent. After Christmas was established, a parallel period of preparation, Advent, was also set. The full Christmas cycle, from the beginning of Advent to the beginning of Lent, took up about a quarter of the year. The full Easter cycle, from Ash Wednesday to Advent, took up the other three quarters.

## *The Saints*

The Greek word *hagios,* which is translated "saint" in the New Testament, refers to the condition of being set apart for a special relationship with a god. Being *hagios* did not necessarily signify extraordinary personal sanctity. You could become *hagios* by membership in a group—the people of Israel are *hagios* in the Torah; Paul refers to the members of the early church as *hagios*.

The first saints to have days on which their deaths—their entry into eternity—were commemorated were the early Christian martyrs. Martyrdom was a kind of mysticism. By subordinating everything that the world valued, even life itself, to the pattern of Christ, a martyr reordered the priorities of the world. The martyr was the surest sign, the surest witness (*martyr* means "witness" in Latin) that there is a larger reality. Martyrs continued to walk on this larger path, even when that path took them to their deaths. The ultimate testimony to the validity of spiritual truth was that people would stake their lives on it.

Martyrdom is not a goal; it is a side effect of faithfulness to the spiritual path. But the notion that one must reverse one's way of being to the extent that one holds even one's own life lightly is the kind of radical shift of perspective that all great religions talk about. No religious tradition, Christianity included, teaches that spiritual growth has to be validated by a brutal execution. There have always been other means and expressions of transformation. In fact, in Christian tradition itself, it's John, the disciple closest to Jesus, who is the only disciple *not* martyred. The cults of the martyrs would eventually take on a kind of lurid sentimentality. But for early Christians, the martyr was a dramatic symbol, an icon of the unseen world, and so an imaginative gateway into eternity. As such, they were incorporated into the Christian year.

The original twelve apostles also became part of the Christian calendar. Although the list of apostles' names varies from book to book in the New Testament, they were among the first saints whose days were observed. Though their feast days are irregularly scattered throughout the year, there is a suggestion in some ancient Christian documents that the twelve were aligned with the astrological signs.

The saints and apostles took up residence in that middle realm of myth, legend, and imagination that the Egyptian, Greek, and Roman gods had recently occupied. Thus they filled a crucial imaginative and spiritual function. The growing calendar of saints' days, the Sanctoral Cycle, was a way that the early Church incorporated indigenous festivals and traditions as it moved into northern Europe. Many saints adopted the gentler traits of old gods. Under the protection and blessing of saints' days, many older celebrations became part of Christendom.

## Meeting the North

But the Year of the Lord did not stop developing at that point. Christianity was about to move north—away from the ancient centers of the human world—away from books, governments, libraries, and theaters. It also moved away from the great temples that had been standing since history began. Away from the olive groves, the vineyards, the desert, the burning sun, the wine-dark sea, and the galleys and fishing boats—the things that had given it its first images and sacraments.

It took those symbols, festivals, and philosophies, gathered from Judea and Egypt, Greece and Rome into the endless dark forests of Europe, Scandinavia, and the British Isles; into fog-shrouded moorlands; rolling green hills; fertile river valleys. It traveled into worlds that were still living in the dreamtime before history. It met Gaels and Saxons, Celts and Vikings, druids and berserkers, trolls and elves. It left behind the urbane gods of the empire for a world of gods more raw and fierce than the classical world had known for centuries.

In the years between the end of Rome and the high Middle Ages, Christianity would take root in the northern lands. It was a very long process, though, not complete even at the end of the first millennium. Like any living thing that takes root and thrives, Christianity drew sustenance from the native soil. By the end of this process, it had created its own distinctive culture, one of the world's high civilizations and also one of its great folk cultures. Both of these were expressed in the ritual calendar of Catholic Europe.

Among the common people, this culture was a genuine hybrid of the indigenous ways of the north with the new faith from the south. Christianity and native belief found much that they recognized in one another, especially—as everywhere—in the rhythms of the year. Much

CHRIST AS THE SUN GOD APOLLO, MID-3RD CENTURY CHRISTIAN MOSAIC. *EARLY CHRISTIANS USED MYTHOLOGICAL IMAGES TO EXPLAIN THE MYSTERY OF CHRIST.*

of what is most human in Christian tradition comes from its encounter with people who gathered around fires to keep warm. No matter where in the world it is celebrated, Christmas is colored by northern European winters. The Feast of All Saints and its eve is still lit orange and red from the glow of Irish bonfires. At the same time, the doctrines and stories of Christ worked their way into indigenous blessings and songs, tales and games, rituals of farming and childbirth.

After the sixteenth century, wave after wave of powerful forces—the Protestant Reformation, rationalism, science, industrialization, urbanization, social reform, capitalism—began to break up the culture of Christian Europe. The breakup took a long time. Much of this culture was still thriving through the nineteenth century. Some of it, notably Christmas, managed to adapt with surprising success. But the two catastrophic European wars of the twentieth century ended folk Christianity as a living culture.

In some ways, this ending was no bad thing. The reforms of the nineteenth century improved living conditions so oppressive we can barely imagine them. Sometimes the old ways were uprooted along with oppressive regimes in the great democratic revolutions. The powerful—the Church first among them—used religious and folk beliefs to manipulate and exploit. The line between colorful beliefs and atrocities could be dangerously vague. Witch trials and pogroms were part of this culture, too.

But in losing a public ritual calendar, Western society lost a large piece of its soul. No human society has ever done without a way to mark ritually the passage of time to quite the degree that we are attempting now. The Christian calendar expressed the spiritual imagination of an entire culture. It could be adapted and used by individuals, from the most powerful to the most marginal, to tune ordinary life to a more spacious and gracious rhythm. It provided a system of spiritual practice for a largely illiterate world. It synthesized elements from the whole human story. It remains to be seen what will replace it.

But the old/new eternal mystery is always there, tugging and pulling under our day-to-day awareness like the sea. Now, as individuals, we can still enter the seasons. "Have peace in your heart," says the Eastern Orthodox prayer, "and thousands around you will be saved." In the same way, by entering the seasons one by one, we may build something new.

FALL

# PART ONE

# FALL

The first lesson that the Year of the Lord teaches is, appropriately, a paradox—it begins as the natural year ends. As such, it teaches us to watch for the signs of a beginning when, to all appearances, the world seems the least promising.

The fall of the year in nature and in the liturgical calendar is a rich and nuanced drama, a perilous and turbulent time, full of conflict, when the seen and unseen worlds come together. The dynamics of the fall of the year have the sweep of a great symphony or an epic poem. From the vast conflict of light and dark, the greater powers of night and quiet emerge.

Savor the word—*fall*. At this time, we watch the fall of the reign of summer, a great triumph moves deep into a darkness full of danger, promise, and mystery. We pass through a wild night of apparitions into a quiet that grows deeper until it is infused with the lights of candles and stars. Time narrows down until it comes to its turning point, as all creation holds its breath in the silent night and waits for the entry of something new and unimaginable.

*St. Michael*, by Raphael (1483-1520). *Michael faces the dragon of darkness at the beginning of fall.*

# 2

# September 29

## Michaelmas:
## The Feast of Michael and All Angels

*Christians have always felt themselves to be attended by healthful spirits—swift, power-*
*ful, and enlightening. Those beneficent spirits are often depicted in Christian art in*
*human form, with wings to signify their swiftness and spacelessness, with swords to*
*signify their power, and with dazzling raiment to signify their ability to enlighten.*

*—Lesser Feasts and Fasts*

*Thou Michael the victorious,*

*I make my circuit under thy shield,*

*Thou Michael of the white steed,*

*And of the bright brilliant blades,*

*Conqueror of the dragon,*

*Be thou at my back,*

*Thou ranger of the heavens,*

*Thou warrior of the King of all,*

*O Michael the victorious,*

*My pride and my guide,*

*O Michael the victorious,*

*The glory of mine eye.*

*I make my circuit*
*In the fellowship of my Saint,*
*On the machair, on the meadow,*
*On the cold heathery hill;*
*Though I should travel ocean*
*And the hard globe of the world*
*No harm can ever befall me*
*'Neath the shelter of thy shield;*
*O Michael the victorious,*
*Jewel of my heart,*
*O Michael the victorious,*
*God's shepherd thou art . . .*

> —Carmina Gaedelica, Hymns and Incantations Col-
> lected in the Highlands and Islands of Scotland in the
> Last Century

## The Experience

Autumn is poignant, so it belongs to the angel who carries a point—the Archangel Michael, who wields sword and spear for the people of God against the powers of darkness. The point of Michael's spear is the poignancy of autumn that pierces our hearts and wakes us from drowsy summer, calling us away with a sharp longing for something else.

We humans see the spiritual beauty of a thing most clearly when its time is passing or passed. Nothing becomes legendary or sacred until it dies. In autumn, nature's time is passing. The world is at its most beautiful and poetic because it is passing away. The natural world lingers for a moment on the brink of this transformation into legend or holiness. It has the bittersweet beauty of something that we are about to lose. The light turns from the clear, practical white light of summer into the mellow gold that we call antique—like the yellowed pages of an old book, the sepia of old photographs, or tarnished brass. Old light, legends of the fall, Indian summer. Nature has one foot over the threshold of eternity and glows with a slant of light from the other side of the door.

Michael is the angel of this transition from time to eternity. The point of his spear is the point where eternity breaks into time and transforms it—both "now, and at the hour of our

*The Angel Standing in the Sun*, by Joseph W. M. Turner (1775-1851). "With wings to signify their swiftness and spacelessness, swords to signify their power, dazzling raiment their ability to enlighten . . ."

death," as the Rosary says. The death of the year, beginning at Michaelmas, acts out this transformation sacramentally.

At the same time, there's a new kind of life in the air. As dead leaves and withered plants shrivel back toward the ground, it's as if their summer life is transformed into the tingling energy of the fall air. This combination of the beautifully dying and the bracingly awake is the unmistakable spiritual atmosphere of autumn. Michael is the patron of the process. The flaming trees say it all. They are a last flare of gorgeousness before death and, at the same time, a signal fire, a wake-up call to the soul. Michael, whose feast is celebrated one week after the autumn equinox, is the lord of autumn, the angel of the flaming trees.

Michael's color is red. In the classical world, people saw Michael in the god Mars—red Mars, iron Mars, warrior Mars. Autumn is when the blood races, red blood full of iron. Throughout autumn, Michael shoots iron arrows into our atmosphere as meteor showers in the northern hemisphere. Meteorites were the most convenient sources of iron for early tool-makers. From it, they fashioned knives, spear points, and arrow points. The Egyptians called this iron "black copper from heaven," and the Sumerians denoted it by two characters repre-senting "heaven" and "fire."

In summer we celebrate our at-homeness in the world. Michaelmas balances that feel-ing. In autumn we feel our not-at-homeness, the sense of wanting something else, something we can't name. We feel like wayfaring strangers. In the African-American spiritual, Michael rows the boat ashore, guiding the crossing of the dark waters. An antiphon from the old Roman liturgy for the dead prays, "May Michael the standard bearer lead them into the holy light." Michael is the guide who leads us through this strange world as he led the Israelites through Sinai, the "great and terrible wilderness." He ferries us across the darkest, most tempestuous time of the year to bring us safely to the beginning of Advent. He guards our hearts through dangerous transitions until the light dawns.

Summer is static—in Latin, *solstice* means "the stationary sun." On summer days, time feels as if it stands still. The Divine is quite close, in the dark shining green of the leaves, the warm soil under our feet, the hum of insects. Summer is a sacrament of natural harmony with God, when we can see that "fallen nature" is really only nature seen with fallen eyes, and that all around us paradise is still going on. Midsummer, as Shakespeare knew, is a time for dreaming.

Autumn is not a dreaming time. In the apocryphal Gospel of Bartholomew, Michael goes with Christ into Hell after the Crucifixion to awaken souls who have fallen asleep. The lesson of Michaelmas is that growth happens when we become more *awake*. In autumn, we fall from the dreaming paradise of summer back into the conflict of light and dark. Conflict is the core of drama, and autumn is a dramatic season. Think about autumn skies and sunsets—the turbulence, color, and sweep, the sheer widescreen seventy-millimeter spectacle of it. There is war in Heaven; you can see it. At the autumn equinox, darkness has fought its way back until it's equal with the light. That's when Michael charges in.

It's easy to forget the menace of the waning year, although every so often—even in our well-lighted and heated homes, with our marvelous systems of food production and distribution—we get a chill that's more than the cold wind. In autumn, our natural protection drains away. We are left to the mercy of the cold and dark and the wild, tumultuous skies. In old Christian Europe, people saw in the autumn skies the Wild Hunt riding to harvest souls. We'd like to think that because we are no longer so vulnerable to winter, the old rhythms have no power over us. But there are still people who hate and fear the coming of the dark. "Seasonal affective disorder" is simply another way of describing the Wild Hunt passing by. Michael does battle with the Wild Hunt. He is the strength that helps us face our fear at the death of nature—to hold on until Christmas.

In Catholic teaching, Michael is the power that stands for us when the natural life of our bodies ebbs away at the hour of death. It's the same at the death of the year. Michael is what we have left when our natural support is taken away, when we get no strength from exterior sources. Michael keeps our backbones as straight as his spear.

Michael presides over the equinox, the time of equal night and day when things hang in the balance. Medieval art often shows Michael holding a pair of balancing scales—just like the Egyptian god Anubis, another lord of transitions and guide of the dead. Those scales are the astrological sign of Libra, which begins a week before Michaelmas. Unlike the spring equinox, when the light is rising, the dark grows stronger in the fall. Autumn has the grandeur and sadness of gods going down to defeat, like the old Norse Twilight of the Gods. But in our story, Michael rescues us at the last moment, as the year ticks down to its zero point. Michael's battle goes from the equinox to the beginning of Advent. It's the final movement of the Christian year, and Michael fights the last battle, just as he does in the Book of Revelation.

When Michael's work is done, there is the sudden stillness of Advent, the silence after the battle. We've passed safely through. The landscape is wasted—like after the passage of armies—but we're still here. The conflict gives way to quiet. After a while, in the distance, a faint new music begins in the bleak, silent landscape—the first carols of Christmas.

*THE WILD HUNT, BY MAURICE SAND, 1851. THE YEAR GROWS OLD AND THE WILD HUNT RIDES, BRINGING IN THE COLD AND DARK.*

Michaelmas is a reminder that autumn is the time to do the spiritual preparation for Advent and Christmas. What kind of work? Michael's role as dragon fighter gives a clue. In stories and dreams, serpents and dragons can symbolize the dark parts of ourselves—instinctive, unconscious, primitive parts we don't want to face. Our dragons are our old, unresolved energies, desires, hurts, and fears—the parts of ourselves we're not aware of that can compel us to act counter to love and growth. If we can look at these dragons in daylight, they begin to lose that power. Michael's spear is a ray of light, the light of awareness, shining on the things that live in the dark. If we can turn this light on our dragons, we can hook them and lift them up into the light. Once seen in the light, we can let them go or turn them from enemies into servants.

St. George, the famous dragon slayer, is a version of Michael. When St. George defeats the dragon, he uses his lady's "girdle"—her belt or sash—to leash the monster and walk him back out of the wilderness. The lady's girdle is a gentle weapon, but it's enough to transform the dragon from a monster into a companion. Michael is the patron saint of the process that very gently and slowly but surely brings parts of us that we thought were dead and buried out of the wilderness and into the light.

We all carry the spear of Michael. Whenever we look straight at anything dark in ourselves we shine a light on it. In the simple act of looking, its power weakens. The grotesque mask drops away and we see it's just us.

## *The Story*

From the time of the first civilizations, humans have had glimpses of a great power who acts as guide, guardian, and warrior for mortals. This power that leads us over the perilous threshold from darkness to light, danger to victory, time to eternity. Different cultures have seen different aspects of this power across the ages. These glimpses make up the story of Michael in history, mythology, and religion.

Along with Gabriel, Auriel, and Raphael, Michael is one of the archangels in ancient Hebrew tradition, the only four angels mentioned by name in the Bible. His name in Hebrew means "Who is like God?" The archangels probably originated in the pantheons of the ancient Near Eastern civilizations—Babylon, Sumer, or Chaldea. Michael is first mentioned in the Bible in Daniel as "one of the chief princes" of the heavenly host and the special guardian of Israel. Tradition says he is the angel who went before the Israelites as a pillar of fire or smoke in Exodus and Joshua.

In Revelation, the last book of the New Testament, Michael is the leader of the heavenly host in the final battle against the dragon, the forces of darkness and chaos. The most ancient layers of the Old Testament contain pieces of a widespread Middle-Eastern myth in which the creator god fights a tremendous battle against the dragon of chaos, who lives in the sea. As Michael gradually became known as God's chief warrior, he took over this struggle in legend and so became the great dragon fighter.

Reverence for Michael and the other archangels was one of the many elements of Judaism retained by the early Christian movement. In the late fifth century, Dionysius the Aeropagite, a Christian mystic and scholar in Syria, developed the classic Christian doctrine of angels, describing their nature, responsibilities, and ranking. Christian teaching associates Michael with Last Things—the end of time and the end of life. As such, he has four main functions: rescuing the souls of the faithful from the power of the enemy, especially at the hour of death; calling human souls away from earth and bringing them to judgment; fighting against Satan; and serving as the champion of God's people.

From the earliest Christian centuries, Michael's cult was popular in the eastern Roman Empire—modern-day Turkey—where the sick invoked Michael for healing. The emperor Constantine built a church in his honor for this purpose near Constantinople. Christians dedicated healing hot springs to Michael in Greece and Asia Minor. Egyptian (Coptic) Christians placed the River Nile under his protection. They observed the archangel's main feast on November 12.

A famous fifth-century apparition of Michael on Monte Gargano in Italy popularized Michael's cult in Europe. His feast date on September 29 is the anniversary of the dedication of a basilica to Michael near Rome. Shrines and churches dedicated to Michael often perch on hills, mountaintops, and other high places, remembering Michael's cosmic battles. Michael's most famous shrine in western Europe is the Benedictine abbey of Mont Saint-Michel in Normandy, founded in the tenth century to commemorate another appearance of the archangel.

Michael's cult spread throughout Europe and became especially popular in the British Isles. By the end of the Middle Ages, the Church had dedicated almost seven hundred sites to Michael in England alone. Well-known sites include St. Michael's Mount in Cornwall, believed to be the location of an eighth-century vision; Skellig Michael in County Kerry, Ireland; and the Church of St. Michael on Glastonbury Tor in Somerset. Michael is the patron saint of Coventry Cathedral, destroyed by German bombers during World War II. Rebuilt, it has become England's most famous modern church building, a symbol of hope rising from destruction.

Michael is the patron of soldiers and in particular of the great knightly orders of the Middle Ages, such as the Knights Templar, stewards of the Temple Mount in Jerusalem. Michael is the angel who appeared to Joan of Arc. He is the patron of horses and often chosen as a patron of cemeteries. For many centuries, Michaelmas was one of the most popular celebrations of the Church Year. In the British Isles, Michaelmas marked the beginning of the hunting season. It was the traditional time for apple picking, brewing cider, and plucking goose down for mattresses and pillows. Goose is a traditional dish for a festive

ST. MICHAEL'S CHURCH, GLASTONBURY TOR, SOMERSET, ENGLAND. *MICHAEL'S SHRINES ARE ON HIGH PLACES, WHERE THE PRINCE OF HEAVEN STANDS GUARD.*

Michaelmas dinner. Because it coincides with the autumn equinox, Michaelmas is one of the four "quarter days" of the calendar, traditionally a day for holding courts and paying rents.

Historian Ronald Hutton describes Michaelmas as "the largest and most dramatic communal rite" of the year for the islanders of the Hebrides, off the west coast of Scotland. They saw Michael as patron of the sea and so, as people who made their living from the sea, they gave him special honor. On Michaelmas Eve, the women of each house baked a huge cake called the *struan* made from all the varieties of grain grown on the farmstead. On Michaelmas morning, after church, families feasted on struan and lamb, with the leftovers given to the poor.

Whole villages then joined in a great horseback procession to the local gravey̲
the priest. The cavalcade would ride sunwise around the graveyard, singing a
Michael—"an annual tribute to the dead," says Hutton, "near the end of the s̲
fishing season and after the harvest." The rest of the day was spent in sports, g̲
horse racing. At night the village gathered for gift giving and dancing.

This traditional "Blessing of the Struan" expresses the mood of the feast:

*Milk and eggs and butter,*
*The good produce of our own flock,*
*There shall be no dearth in our land,*
*Nor in our dwelling.*
*Be thine own sanctuary around us,*
*Ward from us spectre, sprite, oppression,*
*And preserve us.*
*Consecrate the produce of our land,*
*Bestow prosperity and peace,*
*In name of the Father the King,*
*And of the three beloved apostles.*

        —Carmina Gaedelica

## *Entering the Season*

**Letting go of the old**—Go through your home and look for things you can get rid of; likewise look for things in yourself that you can let go. Ask God for courage to release what no longer serves you—possessions, relationships, old habits of thought or behavior.

**Justice**—As President Kennedy said, "Here on earth, God's work must truly be our own." Consider seriously what you might do to help Heaven in the struggle for justice on earth. Is there an organization or a cause you have long considered worthwhile to which you might offer your support?

**The unseen world**—The Christian path calls us to base our lives in something beyond what we perceive with our senses. As the natural world falls away in autumn, the Church looks to the unseen world—specifically, at Michaelmas, to the order of angels. Reaffirm the reality of the unseen in your life. Reflect on the times when you feel you have received guidance or direction, especially those times when the guidance was not apparent at the moment, but perceived in retrospect.

**Autumn leaves**—Take a child to collect red leaves, the color of Michael.

**Practicing awareness**—There are many books describing ways to strengthen your powers of awareness. One good guide is the late Father Anthony de Mello, S. J., in books such as *Sadhana: A Way to God*. Read what the great Eastern Orthodox prayer teachers have to say about "attention" in *The Art of Prayer: An Orthodox Anthology* (Faber & Faber, 1997), edited by Father Timothy Ware.

**Visiting a grave**—Take flowers to the grave of a relative, or to a local cemetery or war memorial. Consider the life of someone you knew or of a public figure who has died recently. Can you see themes or meanings that seem more clear now that this life has finished? Read the last book of Thomas Malory's *Morte d'Arthur*, about the death of Arthur, the "autumn king"; or recall, if you're old enough, the emotions that surrounded the assassination of President Kennedy. Or read Gerard Manley Hopkins' poem "Spring and Fall" to feel the sense of glory passing from the earth through the eyes of a young girl.

**Music**—In its power to make the heart yearn and the blood race, the sound of pipes is the quintessential music of Michaelmas. There are several good CDs of Scottish military bands—look for the Black Watch or the Gordon Highlanders. Or for something a little more subtle, try the fine Scottish pipe band, the Tannahill Weavers.

HALLOWEEN ILLUSTRATION BY W. SMALL, 1890. ALL HALLOWS' EVE WAS LOVED
BEST IN THE GAELIC-SPEAKING PARTS OF THE BRITISH ISLES.

# 3

# OCTOBER 31

## HALLOWEEN

# NOVEMBER 1

## THE FEAST OF ALL SAINTS

# NOVEMBER 2

## THE FEAST OF ALL FAITHFUL DEPARTED

*. . . as imagination bodies forth*

*The forms of things unknown, the poet's pen*

*Turns them to shapes, and gives to airy nothing*

*A local habitation and a name.*

> —William Shakespeare,
>
> *A Midsummer Night's Dream*

*This aye night, this aye night,*

*Every night and all,*

*Fire and sleet and candlelight*

*And Christ receive thy saule.*

> —Anonymous, "The Lyke Wake Dirge"

## The Experience

It is said that, in the dark time of the year, Russian peasants used to regard any stranger approaching the house as an emissary from another world.

Strange associations flap and flutter just beyond the lamplight of human memory—uncanny strangers arriving at our threshold after dark, bringing with them something that disrupts or disturbs, but that also might be a blessing. Such "night visitors" are one of the oldest and most widespread folk motifs of Europe. From Ireland to the frontiers of Asia, since long before the arrival of Christianity, eerie strangers make their nocturnal rounds in the dying months of the year, singing and performing; playing tricks or bearing gifts; begging and blessing; walking, riding, flying. Out of the dark, into the small circle of light from the door, and back into the night they go, in legends and in dreams and in enacted customs on real village streets. Sometimes feared and sometimes welcomed, these wanderers taught the Church something, and the Church taught them something. Through them, and using them both, God entered the October night.

Although some contemporary Christians may be uncomfortable with the knowledge, a few minutes' reflection on the creeds should be enough to remind anyone that Christianity rests on belief in the supernatural. The feasts of All Saints (November 1) and All Faithful Departed (November 2), formerly called All Hallows and All Souls, are the special Christian recognitions of that other world. These feasts remind us that the roots and branches of Christianity are in the unseen, and that the trunk passes for only the littlest while through this daylight world of time and the five senses. They remedy our unease with the unseen, teach us to get along with mystery. They are the answer to our primitive assumption that what is out there in the dark is hostile or evil. They show that something very strange can mean us very well.

Today, even for most practicing Christians, the feasts of All Saints and All Faithful Departed go by with little attention paid, making little difference. The popular holiday of Halloween does make a difference. It is a big event for children and has grown bigger in the course of this century. But not much reflection is generally given to the relationship between Halloween and the Church feasts that are its origin. The two feast days and All Hallows' Eve are not connected like the three days of the Triduum (Good Friday through Easter), or Christmas and its Eve. Nor is the religious meaning of these days clear to most people.

Technically speaking, Halloween is the vigil of All Hallows. Vigils are the night face of the Church. The practice of keeping vigils owes something to the old way of reckoning the day, from sunset to sunset. Days are still counted this way in contemporary Judaism. This way of figuring incorporates the preceding night into the "day" of the feast. Rather than being an interval or interruption, night becomes a vital part of the whole observance. In the two archetypal Christian holidays of Easter and Christmas, it is the vigil that contains the actual transformative event—the moment of the Resurrection at Easter and of Christ's birth at Christmas. The theurgy, the sacred work, takes place at the middle of the night, when the way is open between eternity and this world.

The Gospels suggest that night is the time for teaching the mysteries of the kingdom. "What I say to you in the dark you must repeat in broad daylight," Jesus told his friends. The first Eucharist was performed at night, followed by the mystical "farewell discourses" in John. In a famous nighttime dialogue, Jesus instructed Nicodemus, the seeker Pharisee, in the mysteries of rebirth and the holy spirit.

Vigils did not adapt well to modern times. In fact, they became a little notorious. In the interim between the night vigil and the actual celebration of the feast, people would often go into the streets. These morning intermissions led to public reveling around the church, and officials grew leery. The number of vigils was reduced further and further over the centuries. The Church now reserves the potent nature of night observances to the two great nights, and even Christmas Eve is not technically a vigil but merely a night mass. Today, outside of Christmas and Easter, only All Saints has a vigil still popularly observed, though not, of course, in church. The secularized vigil of All Saints is like an impish little brother to these great vigils, a small echo of their world-transforming mysteries.

Halloween and Christmas are the two great folk expressions in the Church Year of the popular imagination—of the *mens fidele*, the "mind of the faithful." All over Europe, before the Protestant Reformation, the feasts of the Church Year had been rich with popular customs. The Christian vision was incarnated up and down the scale of culture, from scholars creating great structures of intellect and theology, down to the places in the common heart where people dreamed, played, and sang.

Yet, there has always been a strain within the Church that seems to believe that the imagination itself is pagan. This belief became stronger after the Reformation and today, perhaps, strongest of all in the great Protestant empire of the United States. It is as if these Christians secretly believe that the Incarnation is too good to be true and cannot accept that Christ is completely present in human nature. They struggle to hold the Divine apart from life, believing that the sacred is somewhere else—anywhere but here. They seem to fear that if God comes to us through music or green grass or the pictures that old Granny Uncon-scious keeps in her cupboard, God will be soiled.

In fact, the imagination is exactly where the Divine and the human meet. It is the middle world where God's light is softened, diffused, and reflected down to us. When St. Paul says that we now see "as in a glass darkly," the glass he means is a looking glass—a mirror. For all human history, including most of the Christian Era, it was understood that humankind needed mirrors to see and experience the Divine. Mirrors are all those things that reflect God into experience the way the moon reflects sunlight—sacrament, liturgy, festivals, dreams, art, poetry, song, drama, legends, love, vision, myth, saints, angels, gods, magical animals, fair-ies, ghosts, the vision of childhood. (In that sense, it's right that Halloween is for children. The vision of childhood, where so many actions are ritual actions and so many objects reveal the sacred, is naturally sacramental.) For St. Paul and for most humans before and—until relatively recently—since, the zone between humankind and God was not empty. It was a full and busy place, an ornate system for shuttling us up and down the ladder to Heaven.

The unseen world is the realm of vision or creative imagination, of the divine ability of human beings to bring things out of the darkness that reflect God in small and immediate ways. To our senses there is nothing between us and the sky. But holy imagination suffocates in such emptiness. In reaching for a more living connection with God, it fills that empty space with images. This intermediate place is the genuine realm of the supernatural, that is, between nature and God. It is also the domain of the moon, that celestial mirror that stands between us and the sun and reflects its light gently to us, so that human eyes can bear it. It is Mary's domain, the Lady who, in Christian imagination, stands on the crescent moon and mediates light to us.

Most scary stories come out of a rather primitive human reaction to mystery. We want mystery more than anything, but we are thrown off balance by it. The imagination falls short in imagining or describing the sacred thing that is approaching, and so we settle for making it scary. But the spook is simply a stand-in.

A sacrament of the Church is more central, more essential, and more developed than a fairy tale or ghost story, but there's a family resemblance in how these different expressions of the supernatural work. Think of it in terms of biology. A human body is a much more devel-oped organism than a mouse, yet the mouse and the human work in many similar ways. If we can't learn the lessons of the mouse, we will never begin to appreciate the lessons of the human body. Similarly, if we don't understand how art, symbols, metaphors, imagination,

*Jesus Born*, by Albrecht Dürer (1471-1528). Mary in Christian imagery is associated with the moon, the realm that connects heaven and earth.

and stories work in their simpler forms, we'll never understand how they work in their most sublime form in the Christian sacraments.

Mystery is, of course, not specifically Christian. It flows underneath the whole human race and always has. We all share the old sea. Christianity is not a sealed-off inlet. The Church is more like a boat, as it's portrayed in Christian iconography, a vessel for riding the waves and tides, surrounded by the ancient surge and smell of the sea. Our Lady is *Stella Maris*, the Star of the Sea. The Church is a great repository of mystery, but for the last century or so, the face of the mainstream churches have been pretty much the rational, main-street, daylight face of God—theology, ethics, charity, social outreach. Paul would have called it law and works.

Then disaster struck. The churches began hemorrhaging members by the millions. This catastrophe is often blamed on "the sixties," by which people generally mean the liberalization of theology associated with that era. I blame dwindling Church membership on the sixties too, but for a different reason. The sixties awakened a thirst for a face of God that the churches had long since ceded to the arts, folklore, and popular culture—the night side of God.

When we're cut off from the moon, the night, and the waters of mystery, the spiritual world is blinding and blisteringly arid. Mystery refreshes us. Mystery is a cool dark underground stream, a tributary of the river of living water that bubbled up into that well in a dusty Middle-Eastern village where Jesus stopped at midday and spoke to a Samaritan woman. When our roots are sunk into mystery, we flourish like trees planted by a stream.

Periodically, throughout history, the night side of God, the middle realm, becomes identified with evil. Disaster always follows. When you fear and suppress the night, fear and destruction are what you get. When religion, old or new, suppresses the creatures of the night, it ends up chasing witches with horrible literalness—in recent years hunting down satanic nursery school administrators or searching for diabolical messages in children's books or pop songs.

Close your doors to the people in masks, and you're likely to wake up with your windows smeared with soap. Throw open your doors in ancient human hospitality, welcome the uncanny strangers, and they may turn everything upside down, but they will leave a blessing. Follow the example of Abraham, who offered the unsettling outlanders something to eat and found himself entertaining angels unawares. "I stand at the door of the heart and knock," says the Great Stranger.

It's a powerful and wonderful thing that our children still go out into the October night. When we accept and bless this night's witches and monsters, a certain light begins to shine from behind the grotesque masks. You might even think that there are moonlighting angels behind them. On the Eve of All Hallows, the wild little figures out on the dark streets go under the protection of Mother Mary, in her strange silver light, and in the company of the faithful departed, who come out this night to play.

## *The Story*

In traditional cultures, the important turning points of the year—solstices and equinoxes, or the changes of the pastoral seasons when the herd or flock was let out into summer pasture or brought down for the winter—were understood to stand outside of time. In the more sensuous awareness of time that people had in the absence of precise measuring systems, it was apparent that at these moments, one "time" had ended. Time would start again with the new season, but between the end of one cycle and the beginning of the next was a gap.

At these points, it was believed, the world reverted to the way it was before time began—at the creation, or in the dreamtime, as Australian aborigines say. Our world became continuous with the timeless world. All those beings and powers, the seen and unseen inhabitants of the world before, above, or outside of time—gods, angels, ancestors, spirits—were then present. The pattern also holds true for the miniature year that is the day. The two crucial turning points of the day, midnight and noon, are felt in many traditions, including Christianity, to be smaller cracks in time—midnight, for instance, being the "witching hour." On the psychological level, at these transition points, a barrier between the daylit world of conscious awareness and the huge unknown of the unconscious temporarily falls. Such occasions are perilous, undetermined, turning points and crises, when things can go one way or another.

This human sense of time is so deep and apparently universal that it has found its way into almost every religious tradition. It is the root of most holy days and the source of sacred time. Of course, the timeless can break through at any moment of life. Holy days are simply celebrations and sacraments of that fact.

In the Celtic lands of pre-Christian Europe, a major festival called Samhain was celebrated at the beginning of November to mark the start of winter. This great feast was one of the open places in time. In fact, it seems to have been felt as distinctly more charged and uncanny than the other Celtic seasonal holidays. Perhaps this special charge was because of the feast's setting, in the fall when nights are lengthening. In north Wales, the festival was called *Nos Galan Gaea,* "Winter's Eve." As the realm of the comfortable daylight world grows smaller, the space of the dark and the unknown increases.

In Wales, people sang songs like this:

*A Tail-less Black Sow*
*On Winter's Eve,*
*Thieves coming along*
*Knitting stockings.*

Or in Scotland:

*Halloween will come, will come,*
*Witchcraft will be set a-going.*
*Fairies will be at full speed*
*Running in every pass.*
*Avoid the road, children, children.*

In later centuries, the European Church set the feasts of All Hallows and All Souls—in honor, respectively, of all the saints and all the Christian dead—at exactly the same time as Samhain. It's not clear exactly how the Christian and pagan feasts are related to each other. What we do know is that after the Christian feast was introduced, customs associated with both traditions intertwined to make these days one of the great folk-Christian festivals of Europe.

Anthropologists and folklorists of the nineteenth century theorized that the Christian feasts were set at this time to replace Samhain. They thought that Samhain had been a pagan festival of the ancestral dead and that this association accounted for the Church's special remembrance of the dead at this time. As historians look at the evidence today, this interpretation seems less certain. For one thing, from the oldest references to Samhain it's not clear that the feast was connected with the dead. On the other hand, Samhain was associated with just about every other kind of supernatural entity. And in folklore, there is an obvious and ancient imaginative tendency to confuse or merge the human dead with fairies and other supernatural beings.

Another problem in connecting the two festivals is that the first churches to celebrate the feast of All Hallows on November 1 were not located in those countries where Samhain traditions were strongest: Ireland, Scotland, and Wales. Instead the Christian feast was instituted in England and Germany in the early eighth century. Moreover, it was not until centuries later, around the year 1000, that the Christian feast of the dead, All Souls, was set on November 2.

Still, the coincidence of the dates begs some explanation. Laying Christian festivals on pagan feast days was an established practice. It may be that, instead of replacing a pagan feast of the dead, the Church's motive was to provide a Christian set of supernatural beings—the saints—to displace the motley crew of heathen entities that gathered around old Samhain. Perhaps this motivation is why Pope Gregory IV in 835 so strongly urged the Holy Roman Emperor, Louis the Pious, to institute All Hallows across Europe. Later, All Souls might have been paired with the older holy day to emphasize the Christian doctrine of the communion of all believers, living and dead.

Whatever its origin, this pair of medieval feasts certainly had an uncanny and superstitious aura from the start. In early records of this festival, the departed do play a central role, but whether this association comes from pagan memory or Christian theology is impossible to know for sure. What is undeniable is that there's a coincidence and mingling of moods between Samhain and All Hallows/All Souls. It's worth taking a look at the process of how the festival developed over time, because, along with Christmas, All Hallows' Eve is the outstanding example of the hybridization of European native tradition and Christian teaching.

While the days of All Hallows and All Souls were mostly occupied with liturgical celebrations inside the church, the Eve of All Hallows was a marriage of the old and new. We don't know exactly what the pagan British actually did to observe Samhain, but some things stand out by their persistence in the traditions. Fire—bonfires especially—played a part. Divination, telling the future, did too. Feasting and merrymaking took place, along with guising or mumming (going from dwelling to dwelling in some kind of costume, along with ritualized begging and sometimes the enactment of simple drama).

The specifically Christian contribution to the mood of the season is not always acknowledged, but it is significant. The records of Christian All Hallows carry that distinctive Halloween combination of somberness, delicious fear, and firelit festivity. By the high Middle Ages, All Saints and All Souls were spectacularly theatrical celebrations, all black velvet, gilt, and torchlight. In 1539, the church of St. Mary Woolnoth in London, as Ronald Hutton recounts, "paid five maidens wearing garlands to play harps by lamplight"—potent Halloween atmospherics indeed.

Ghosts may be an entirely Christian contribution to Halloween. For certain, All Souls provided its own set of dramatic terrors, especially since it was introduced in a period in which the imagination of the Church was dwelling more and more on Hell and stressing the doctrine of Purgatory. When the Church taught that prayers could influence the condition of a soul in Purgatory, it was in effect saying that the barrier between this world and the next was permeable. Purgatory brought the dead much closer; they are not wholly departed for their permanent dwellings. As these ideas filtered into the popular culture, they strengthened the sense of being linked across time with departed loved ones at this season. So it may be that our Halloween ghosts and devils first came steaming out of the parish church.

When the Protestant Reformation swept away Purgatory, All Souls, and masses for the dead, this old association was too strong in people's minds to be swept along with them. When families could no longer pray for their departed in church, they went outdoors, to patches of wasteland that became known as Purgatory Fields. There we can sense another familiar Halloween atmosphere. Farm families out on the heath would light a bundle of straw on the end of a pitchfork and pray for their dead while it burned. In the dreamy way of tradition, this custom sometimes drifted back into the pre-Christian habit of walking the fire in sunwise circles around the fields to ask for protection and blessing.

As the centuries went by, because of the legacy of Samhain, the folk celebration of All Hallows and its eve was most energetic in Ireland and in areas influenced by Irish immigration. The observance began to fade from old strongholds in Wales and central Scotland, but with the mass nineteenth- and twentieth-century Irish diaspora into England and America, it took on a new life that ensured its survival. Halloween today is a wonderful example of an extremely old custom, with roots in pre-Christian Europe, that has been celebrated without a break to this day, and that, unlike many other traditions, never really needed to be revived.

Trick-or-treating, the centerpiece of Halloween as we know it, came into America and England with the Irish immigration. Trick-or-treating is the sturdiest descendant of the many variations of door-to-door ritualized begging/performing/mischief-making that can be found all over Europe. Historically, this complex of traditions is even more associated with the Christmas cycle; it lingers in a gentler form as caroling. Just below the surface, there's an evocative exchange of motifs between Christmas and Halloween. In his recent book, *The Battle for Christmas*, historian Stephen Nissenbaum describes how alarm over raucous, sometimes destructive, house-to-house merrymaking by groups of young men in the early nineteenth century was a factor in making Christmas the more domestic, indoor celebration we know today. The conflict between post-World War II house-proud suburbanites and the "trick" aspect of American trick-or-treating led to a similar shift. As trick-or-treating is moved more and more off the streets into daylight hours, sometimes even to the nearest weekend to accommodate busy moms and dads, we can see a similar desire to contain and juvenilize the tradition.

Old records from Europe show us that the proud antecedents of trick-or-treating were anything but juvenile. We hear about the Welsh *Mari Llwyd* (the Grey Mare), a real horse's skull with a snapping jaw and bottle-bottom eyes, mounted on a pole and hung around with a white sheet to conceal the operator, who carried the grimly yammering apparition from door to door. Men called "hags," with masked faces and wearing sheepskins or old ragged clothes, frightened those out walking late. "Soul-caking" boys in women's clothes with blackened faces floated happily into any kitchen, making cheeky conversation with householders as they ate and drank whatever they found.

Historian Carlo Ginzburg has linked these pan-European traditions with a body of stories and beliefs about a host of the dead, or other supernatural beings, who ride the skies or roam the earth in the late months of the year. In northwestern Europe, the most famous of these hosts was the Wild Hunt (we've met them already in connection with Michaelmas). Sometimes their leader is Odin, king of the Norse gods. Sometimes he is King Arthur, or another mythical British character, Herne the Hunter. In other traditions, the leader is the Devil, or an old woman called Perchta or Holda. In different interpretations, the Night Wanderers have different functions. Sometimes they are on God's side—they pursue the Devil across the sky, or they battle for the health of the crops. Sometimes they are deadly evil— they kidnap children or other unwary souls. There are many stories about humans unlucky enough to encounter the Wild Hunt in some lonely place on a winter night. In some variations, the wanderers visit human homes—sometimes to leave a blessing, sometimes to work mischief, sometimes to abduct the living. Ginzberg speculates that both the myths and the acted-out traditions may be related to an ancient form of shamanistic religion practiced in eastern Europe.

Since trick-or-treaters have such an interesting pedigree, what about jack-o'-lanterns? They are also part of the Irish celebration, though they are found in some places in England as well. In fact, the name *jack-o'-lantern* comes from the eastern counties of England. The term was used first for the glowing lights people could sometimes see over marshes at night—

gas from decaying vegetation that momentarily ignited; in stories, such lights became wandering spirits. "I am that merry wanderer of the night," says Puck, the mischievous fairy in Shakespeare's *A Midsummer Night's Dream*. So was Jack-o'-Lantern, also known as *puca*, an Old English world for "devil," the source, in fact, of the name "Puck." In Britain, jack-o'-lanterns were carved out of turnips or squashes and were literally used as lanterns to guide guisers on All Hallows' Eve. Like illuminated gargoyles floating in the night, jack-o'-lanterns both protected and frightened. They were useful for young men impersonating spirits of the dead, floating, apparently disembodied, around cottages at night and peering mischievously through windows.

As the new church holidays put down roots into European culture, they mingled with firelit, game-playing, reeling Samhain. The pagan festival became a shadowy partner to the Church feast, while the Christian holidays helped keep the old customs alive. As the two worked together, the old traditions and stories became the new body of the Christian holy day, fleshing it out, giving it a richness of mood and meaning that extended from the Church into the cottages and firesides, heaths, fields, and village streets. In turn, Christian theology gave the native customs a vitality that they had not had, perhaps, since the last druid hopped a ship for Brittany one step ahead of Roman spears.

All Hallows worked like a small-scale Christmas, pulling indigenous customs into orbit around it. Without All Hallows, Samhain might have dwindled into mere high jinks and superstition, eventually disappearing. With All Hallows and All Souls, Samhain was resurrected as Halloween. The age-old feeling for Winter's Eve was solemnized in the Church's belief in the Communion of Saints, the living relationship across time and death of all souls in Christ. Halloween and All Hallows/All Souls were, thus, two scenes of one drama. They divided the day and night of the feast between them, the eve going to the popular drama; the day, to the liturgical one.

Protestant reformers didn't care much for either production and abolished what they could control—the elaborate liturgical celebration. The Reformation found All Saints a tough nut to crack, but All Souls was scotched for good in the sixteenth century, partly because of abuses such as money offerings for souls in Purgatory. All Souls was kicked out of church, but it continued to influence the popular holiday in a persistent sense of the presence of the dead. Halloween carried the faithful departed along for all the centuries that they were no longer welcome in church. In return, because of the centuries during which the Eve of All Hallows meant the Mass of the Dead and tolling bells at midnight, Halloween lived on strengthened with Christian love and mystery that made the night, even dressed in outlandish rags and blackface, alive with holy spookiness. The good Christian folk forced out into the fields to comfort their ancestors' souls met the wild boys with their jack-o'-lanterns, and a compact was made. That unity enabled the feast to survive.

The Christian feasts of All Saints and All Faithful Departed are not complete without their shadowy eve, any more than Easter or Christmas are without theirs. Today the Church is beginning to see this small cycle of feasts as a trove of symbols to awaken the Christian sense of the continuity of the seen and unseen worlds.

## *Entering the Season*

**Church**—The heart of this autumnal cycle is All Saints' Sunday, one of the Seven Principal Feasts of the Church. Though not universally observed, the Episcopal *Book of Occasional Services* now includes a liturgy for All Hallows' Eve as well.

**Trick-or-Treating**—People who research these things have found that the wave of Halloween horror stories in the seventies and eighties about widespread tampering with candy, etc., had little basis in fact. Walk with your children if you feel you should, but let them have the experience of the dark autumn streets, the glow from neighbors' doors, and the strange carnival sensation of gratuitous hospitality suddenly pouring from all these houses.

**Fire**—If you have a fireplace, light the first fire of the year or, better yet, make a bonfire outdoors. Halloween is a time for gathering. Bring friends together around the fire and tell ghost stories.

**The Communion of Saints**—The Christian meaning of these feasts focuses on the communion of all souls in Christ, here on earth and departed. Say prayers for your dead. Set out pictures of those you want to remember and light a candle for each, or burn some incense. Set a place for the departed at the table. Tell stories about them. Bring out a possession of theirs to set in the center of the celebration.

**Dreaming**—The night side of God includes the way God whispers from the unconscious—in imagination, intuition, and dreams. Father John Sanford, a psychotherapist and Episcopal priest, has written a number of good books about the Christian use of dreams as an aid to spiritual growth, including *Dreams: God's Forgotten Language* (Harper San Francisco, 1989).

## *Reading*

Ray Bradbury is the poet of October. His *The Halloween Tree* (Knopf, 1999) is meant for young readers. *Something Wicked This Way Comes* (Avon, 1998) is about the reality of evil, the power of love, childhood's end, and the mystery within familiar things. It is not explicitly about Halloween, but it has Halloween coursing through it.

*The Oxford Book of English Ghost Stories* (Oxford University Press, 1989) is an elegant collection of tales. Roderick Hunt's *Ghosts, Witches, and Things Like That* (Oxford University Press, 1995) may be the best all-purpose Halloween book for young people.

Emily Herman's *Hubknuckles* (Random House, 1985) is a simple, atmospheric Halloween story for children about the mystery of love.

C. S. Lewis's *The Discarded Image*: *An Introduction to Medieval and Renaissance Literature* (Cambridge University Press, 1994) is an engagingly written tour through the preindustrial worldview.

*Stag in the Moonlight*, by William Morris Hunt, ca. 1857.
*Nature feels the coming of the stillness of midwinter.*

# 4

# THE SUNDAY NEAREST ST. ANDREW'S DAY (NOVEMBER 30)

## ADVENT: THE CLOSE AND HOLY DARKNESS

*They watch for Christ*

*who are sensitive, eager, apprehensive in mind,*

*who are awake, alive, quick-sighted . . .*

*who look for him in all that happens, and*

*who would not be surprised,*

*who would not be over-agitated or overwhelmed,*

*if they found that he was coming at once . . .*

*This then is to watch:*

*to be detached from what is present, and*

*to live in what is unseen . . .*

—John Henry Newman

*Good news; But if you ask me what it is, I know not;*

*It is a track of feet in the snow,*

*It is a lantern showing a path,*

*It is a door set open.*

—G. K. Chesterton

*The child wonders at the Christmas Tree:*
*Let him continue in the spirit of wonder*
*At the Feast as an event not accepted as a pretext;*
*So that the glittering rapture, the amazement*
*Of the first-remembered Christmas Tree,*
*. . . May not be forgotten in later experience,*
*In the bored habituation, the fatigue, the tedium,*
*The awareness of death, the consciousness of failure . . .*
*So that before the end, the eightieth Christmas*
*(By "eightieth" meaning whichever is last)*
*The accumulated memories of annual emotion*
*May be concentrated into a great joy . . .*
　　　　　　　—T. S. Eliot,
　　　　　　　　"The Cultivation of Christmas Trees"

## *The Experience*

Like most of us, I used to think that what children liked about Christmas were the presents. I was ignoring the evidence of my own experience. Whoever had a Christmas morning that matched Christmas Eve? I now think that what children (and adults) really like about Christmas is the waiting. Or Advent, to give the waiting its technical name.

Advent is the beginning of the Christian year, when the project of undoing time begins. One of the uses of the Christian year is to train our spiritual senses to see sacraments everywhere, at any time, to see all experience as potentially revealing something of God to us. We can and should use Advent—waiting for Christmas—as a way of knowing more of God more deeply.

I don't mean using Advent as is often done in Sunday-school classes, where a teacher tries to direct a child's actual experience toward some explicitly religious idea or image. For instance, telling children that their Advent excitement is "really" about Baby Jesus in the manger. This is simply making one sacrament—the experience of Advent—point to another: the holy child of Bethlehem. The confusion that results has nipped many spiritual lives in the bud. It's equivalent to holding up a map of a child's favorite vacation spot and telling her that she ought to feel about the map the way she feels about the beach. Everyone can sense that this way of teaching children about God is wrongheaded, though few may be able to say exactly why. But all too often, a child who has been through years of such instruction comes to decide that there isn't much in church for her, or worse, grows into an adult who sits in the pew year after year, dispirited but determined to keep the church thing going.

This sort of Sunday school talk doesn't, and can't, tell us what we're waiting for in Advent, any more than a map can tell us why we want to go to the beach. The proper use of a sacrament is to let it tell us what it is about. The Advent complex of season, liturgy, custom, and music has been worked out over a long time to evoke an experience of the Divine. It's all there; it's wonderfully designed. The Church Year calls on a library of experiences stored deep in memory. Like a composer, it evokes and orchestrates these deep feelings and associations into a melody.

Advent calls on us to take seriously the knowledge of childhood—knowledge from the quiet that winter nights lay over the world and the dark purity of the sky and the polished stars. It is about what you knew in the silence of the waiting woods and in the twinkling white lights that shivered and flickered on bushes and trees as if the world were putting on elegant clothes. Indoors, there was the growing fullness that pressed in all around you like cotton, the glittering hushed midnight excitement, and the tender golden sadness of the music that was also full of that presence.

This quiet but electric expectancy gives us a hint of what it means to wait for Christ. "It's what I always wanted," we hope to hear children say on Christmas morning. My guess is that what they always wanted—and what we always want—comes earlier. What children feel during Advent isn't just squirming impatience for a time that's not here yet. They also sense that daily life is being slowly transformed into something more interesting, something with a story to it. One day in Advent, we cross a threshold that separates ordinary, less meaningful time from something trembling with meaning.

This feeling may be caused by the prospect of boxes under the tree. If so, it's a striking example of how something very big can be induced by a very small and humble stimulus, like the grain of sand in an oyster that makes a pearl. This awareness that's being created is the essence of festival, a golden pattern settling over the familiar world and drawing it up into a new shape. The magic of Advent is like going to bed in the familiar world and waking up in a story. This is part of what we mean by *adventus*, waiting for Christ.

One of the greatest historical trick-or-treats that God ever played on humans is that Christ did not come back to wrap up history in the late first century, as the early Christians expected. Christ's imminent return was the cornerstone of their faith. That it never happened was God's Zen koan. If you're sure that God is going to establish his presence once and for all in a huge crashing Cinemascope Second Coming and it doesn't happen, then where is God? At that point you have to find a different way to think; you have to look in a different direction. Somewhere around the time that Christians finally dropped the expectation of God's immediate return, they began to celebrate Christmas. Advent tells us that in the waiting is somehow the finding.

Is Advent, then, a cosmic bait and switch, a promise that is never fulfilled? It might be, if Advent was the kind of waiting we do in profane time, waiting for a future event that promises to reveal everything. But Advent is not ordinary waiting. Its purpose is to teach us to let go of the hope of finally having. Watching for Christ doesn't mean looking ahead toward the future. Rather, it means looking outside of time or into our hearts, which is, after all, the direction from which Christ comes. It also means looking at the present with wide and attentive eyes. As John Henry Newman said, they wait for Christ who would not be overly distressed to hear that he is coming now. Newman wasn't thinking about people who are so holy that the thought of judgment doesn't disturb them. He was thinking about people who would not be distressed by the end of time, because they know they will never find their heart's desire inside it.

Something comes into the world during Advent. When you bring a Christmas tree indoors, for a while it holds the cold outside air. You can feel it among the branches. Something has crossed your threshold from the outside world into the inside world of your home. This big, dark-green thing with branches sticking out in every direction makes an opening, a channel between two realms of the imagination.

Advent is about the *numinous*, the felt sense of the Divine or supernatural. C. S. Lewis described the numinous as the difference in our response between hearing that there is a tiger in the next room and hearing that there is a ghost in the next room. That difference in the quality of the fear is the presence of the numinous. The perception of the numinous is a very old human capacity that reveals our spiritual senses to be as innate as our animal senses. Our ancestors' hair stood up not only when they sensed carnivores in the dark, but when they sensed gods. The numinous gives us goose bumps, even when there's no danger, even when what's out there is something very, very good. The Bible is full of examples of this feeling. At the sound of the angels, the shepherds were sore afraid with "the great joy that is also a great fear," as T. S. Eliot says in "The Cultivation of Christmas Trees."

The Year of the Lord starts getting numinous around All Saints, but Advent refines this sensation. In Advent, there is not just a ghost but an angel in the next room. Advent is a dramatization of the big truth that there is always something waiting, lurking just beyond the curtains of routine and distraction. Numinousness is the response that our senses register to the near approach of God, but not to God smack in front of our noses. The object of numinous perception is not right here. It is always "in the next room," just about to appear. It is always coming, always Advent. By patient, loving, watchful attendance, the mystery will, "in the fullness of time," make itself known. Time will come to term and deliver eternity.

The pregnancy of Mary is, of course, the gospel image of Advent. Where Michaelmas is poignant, Advent is pregnant. Instead of Michaelmas's chivalric striving, the mood of Advent is the expectancy of the mother. At Michaelmas the spirit goes out into the colorful, tragic peril of the world. During Advent we stay close to home. There is a quiet sureness with Advent, a hush as the great processes move. We feel in our hearts what is coming. The attention turns inward, into what Dylan Thomas called the close and holy darkness.

Einstein said that the fairest thing we can experience is the mysterious, and he was right. On the intellectual level, a mystery is something we don't understand but that we will, or at least can, understand. Advent mystery is not the kind that we don't understand; it's the kind we *can't* understand. But we can know it. The icon of Advent is candlelight in darkness. The light in the center of the darkness is the light of the heart. To the mind, mystery is an impenetrable darkness. But what is dark to the mind is light in the heart. The watchfulness of Advent creates spiritual perceptiveness that is only possible when the mind is quiet and waiting.

In prayer as it's taught in the Eastern Church, attention is drawn away from the exterior world and focused in the heart. At Advent, the life of the world has drawn back inside. In these days of early winter, the light-infused world of summer shrinks until it is condensed into the fire on the hearth, a candle in a window, pinpoint white lights on trees that are darker than the night around them. As Thomas Merton wrote:

> . . . *minds as meek as beasts,*
> *Stay close at home in the sweet hay;*
> *And intellects are quieter than the flocks that feed*
> *by starlight.*

The earth in its turning has balanced its axis squarely on the sun. The sun, which creates our time by its journey across the sky, barely moves. The long days of summer have focused as narrowly as they can. We are approaching the still point of the turning world, and the world knows it.

One Advent, I got up early on a Saturday and took our dog out for a walk. A dusting of snow blew back and forth across the sidewalk. I could hear a neighbor's wind chimes. We went into the woods down the railroad tracks from our house. As we came out into a clearing by a gully, the woods were completely quiet. Even the crows were quiet. The only sound was the creaking of the trees in the wind. Off on the hill on the other side of the gully were two children. I could see the bright colors of their jackets flickering between the gray trees.

The sense of waiting was thick. Something enormous was developing. The stillness was not an absence of activity; it was taut. The woods were holding themselves still, in "a passion of patience," as Charles Williams said. They felt like an empty room waiting for someone to come in. I don't think the woods always felt that way at this time of year. I think that all the Advents that people had ever experienced were working together to create that moment, to wear away a weak spot in time.

In the early winter woods or down the empty streets of your neighborhood in the iron December wind, you can still feel the big thing that's coming, an unbroken thread of feeling from your earliest childhood. On the time line, your childhood is behind you. But in the Year of the Lord, you've come around to the point on the spiral where all your Advents are layered one on top of the other. As it was in the beginning—in your beginning—it is now and ever shall be. Jesus said we have to become as little children to enter the Kingdom of Heaven. With every turning year, the invitation comes again.

## *The Story*

In the view of early Christians, it was the events of the Passion story—the Last Supper, Crucifixion, and Resurrection—that made the difference in history and human nature. The other actions of Jesus' adult ministry were of secondary importance, and his birth may not have been religiously important at all.

As noted in chapter 1, it took some time for the birth of Jesus to be understood as an eternal or supernatural event with spiritual meaning in the lives of Christians. This understanding wasn't fully hammered out until the Council of Chalcedon in the fifth century.

During those years, Christian authorities suggested a number of dates for Jesus' birth. In the fourth century, the Church established December 25 as a universal feast. With Easter as a model, the Church developed a period of spiritual preparation, similar to Lent, before Christmas. The first record of a set season of preparation for Christmas comes from the late fifth century in Gaul (France), where the bishop of Tours decreed a three-day fast each week between November 11, the Feast of Saint Martin, and Christmas. The practice quickly spread through Europe. In various places, Advent began as early as September 24, or as late as December 1. But in general, the period was conceived as a long and rigorous fast, harsh in both the outer and inner worlds. Searching for a theological theme to deepen the spiritual meaning of Advent, the Gallic church focused on the second Advent—the Second Coming of Christ. Judgment and self-examination became Advent themes.

In Rome itself there had already been some festive preparation for the sacred birth. But there was a difference in tone between the northern period of preparation and what took place further south, a difference that has affected the mood and meaning of Advent ever since. Records show that Roman observances had a very different atmosphere from the "winter Lent" of northern Europe. In Rome, Advent was a festive season, perhaps colored by the old Roman December festival of Saturnalia.

When the warm Latin joy over the human birth met the ascetic northern preparations for the supernatural Second Coming, something new developed. Superficially, the fast was made shorter and more lenient. The third Sunday of Advent—Gaudete Sunday—was set aside for a foretaste of Christmas. And in the scriptural readings of the Advent liturgy, themes of joyful expectation began to outbalance the fearful.

By the twelfth century, the two contrasting impulses had begun to create a synthesis, a balancing point for the season. The pull between the affectionate backward look and the anxious forward look—both situated in the world of human time—opened up the present moment. Advent gradually came to focus on preparation for Christ's coming in human hearts. The human birth in the past became a glowing icon of this present birth in the heart. The anticipation of the Second Coming became a reminder to be aware and awake in every moment, watching for the intrusion of the Divine. The tension of moods made the distinctive Advent atmosphere—quietly electric, a joyful suspense.

Advent does not end until the moment of midnight on Christmas Eve. Technically, then, many of our Christmas customs are Advent customs. These include the use of evergreens and other plants that stay green in winter—holly, laurel, yew, ivy, and the oak parasite, mistletoe. These greens are gifts of the north. The strange survival of summer green in the snows had always been a sacrament of the hope for new life through the winter. Decorating dwellings with greenery at midwinter goes back at least as far as there are written records of northern peoples. In a famous directive to missionaries in the seventh century, Pope Gregory the Great instructed them to tolerate such customs and dedicate them to Christ. Gregory's letter set a pattern that allowed many of these traditions to be incorporated into the culture of Christendom.

The use of evergreens seems to be especially a Germanic tradition. By the late fifteenth century, the festive evergreens had taken on the form of the Christmas tree and the Advent wreath. Both customs spread rapidly through northern Europe and, by way of German immigration, into the British Isles and the United States.

It comes as a surprise to realize that the Christmas tree was not widely established as a holiday custom outside Germany until the nineteenth century, and in some parts of Europe and America, not until the twentieth. Indirectly, the pedigree of Christmas trees goes much further back, by way of midwinter greenery, into prehistory. Pagan veneration of trees is well known, and trees loom large in ancient mythologies. Did pre-Christian Germans set up and decorate evergreen trees indoors at midwinter? There's no evidence of it; by all available accounts, Christmas trees don't even seem to have been a medieval custom. But the decorated trees that show up in written accounts around the turn of the sixteenth century must have come from somewhere. As with other Christian customs, people probably fashioned a new creative response to the holiday from bits of ancient custom. As with so many similar things, the result was a resonant new harmony.

The Advent wreath—four equidistant candles forming a cross of light in a circle of evergreen—seems to have been introduced along with the Christmas tree, though it has never become as popular. The older Advent wreaths could be quite large. Suspended from the ceiling, they were reminiscent of British "kissing boughs," large, bowl-shaped frames of greenery suspended from the ceiling, hung with ribbons and gilded fruits. In their circularity, wreaths suggest eternity, and eternity breaking into time is the theme of Advent. The lighting of the wreath's candles is traditionally accompanied by a simple ceremony. On the evening of the first Sunday of Advent, all the lights in the house are extinguished. The youngest child lights the first candle, and there is a simple service of a reading, a prayer, and an Advent hymn. On each of the four Sundays of Advent, an additional candle is lit. As the days move towards Christmas, the light slowly grows.

The days before Christmas are held to be especially perilous ones, as the darkness gathers to its greatest power, and the old year and the new are balanced at a delicate crisis point. In old Europe, all kinds of supernatural creatures thronged in the air at this time of year. The Wild Hunt was especially likely to ride on December nights. The cluster of customs and beliefs that we met at Halloween takes on more benign forms during Advent. The Hunt seems to be distantly related to the supernatural midwinter gift-bringers like St. Nicholas, Knecht Ruprecht, La Befana, and the Christkindl or "Christ Child" (not Christ, but a sort of amalgam of angel and elf who brings gifts in Germany). Other Advent visitors include wassailers, bringing their bowl of spiced ale from house to house; mummers with their strange little drama of St. George and the Black Knight; and the "waits," strolling bands of amateur musicians, ancestors of carolers.

In many ways, Halloween and Christmas are dark and light sisters, two related movements in one composition. The rising dark that Halloween explores is a theme that continues through midnight on Christmas Eve. In Great Britain, Christmastime is traditionally the time for ghost stories (this was one of the Christmas traditions that Charles Dickens helped repopularize). As we've seen, the boundaries between worlds grow thin at the turning point of the year, and all manner of spirits are allowed to pass back and forth more easily than usual. Ghosts throng from Halloween through the time of the holy birth. Hamlet's murdered father walks the ramparts of Elsinore at Christmastime. These apparitions are not always fearful. The community of living and dead, the dominant theme of Halloween, becomes a strand of the Christmas celebration. The custom of setting an extra plate at Christmas dinner for the "uninvited guest" or for a particular saint is a memory of the welcome for departed ancestors we saw at Halloween.

The Church has a number of minor feasts in the days of Advent. Santa Claus is part of this time, at least in the form of his most direct predecessor, St. Nicholas of Holland, whose feast day is December 6.

His story has been told many times. Nicholas was an early Christian saint, Bishop of Myra in Turkey, who lived from the late third through the middle fourth century CE. In legend he became famous for acts of charity. He saved the three daughters of an impoverished nobleman from being sold into prostitution or slavery by throwing a bag of gold, one for each daughter, through their windows on three nights in succession, to provide their dowries. He brought back to life three boys who had been murdered by an evil innkeeper, cut up and pickled in wooden barrels, to be served to unwary guests. He became the patron saint of children, among a wide variety of other groups and trades, including sailors and pawnbrokers.

As he moved into northern Europe with the Church, he took on the tasks of the winter gift bringer, particularly in the Netherlands, where he would make his nighttime visit on December 6. His memory seems to have faded among the Dutch colonists in the New World, but it was revived by a group of literary gentlemen in New York in the early nineteenth century that included Washington Irving and, occasionally, a professor of Oriental and Greek literature named Clement Clarke Moore. Moore is the author of "An Account of a Visit from St. Nicholas," and from that point on, Santa Claus absorbed all the gift bringers that various immigrant groups had brought to America.

Our "letters to Santa" which we may think are artifacts of modern Christmas greed, go back at least four centuries. On St. Nicholas' Day, children would leave letters for the angels to carry to St. Nicholas. As the patron of children, St. Nicholas was also the sponsor of another medieval Christmas custom, the tradition of electing a "boy bishop" from among cathedral choristers. For a brief moment, children ruled over the mighty medieval Church hierarchy. This reversal of roles, the turning upside down of ordinary social structures, is found in many forms in the Christmas season. The French Feast of Fools began as a similar inversion of Church order, this time with the junior clergy taking charge. The Lord of Misrule, a person chosen to oversee and enforce the overthrow of order, became a fixture in courts, aristocratic households, and universities. These figures seem to be the legacy of a very ancient impulse, following closely Roman Saturnalia customs, and even more archaic traditions.

In central Europe, St. Thomas the Apostle—the Doubting Thomas of the Gospels—helps to drive away midwinter demons on his feast day of December 21. In another echo of Halloween, figures in costume roam through the villages, making as much noise as possible on these "Rough Nights." In Greece, noisemaking is used to keep away the *kallikrantzoi*, hideous demons that roam free until Christmas, impersonated by young men in terrifying masks.

As at other crucial times of year, the fields and herds needed protection. Thus many rites for protection, blessing, and purification were carried out at this season. The red-berried holly prevented fairies from entering the house. Farmers created protection around their farms with incense and holy water. Rites like these dramatize keeping guard against negative influences, purifying and quieting the inner atmosphere in preparation for Christmas.

Then there is Lucy. The figure of St. Lucy, as it developed in far northern Europe, is another example of the way that indigenous images fused with Christian lore. Lucy was a fourth-century Italian martyr. Her original name, Lucia, contains the Latin root *lux*, or "light." Perhaps not coincidentally, the date of her commemoration was set for December 24, the winter solstice at that time. As late as the seventeenth century, poet John Donne penned "A Nocturnal Upon S. Lucies Day," which, as he noted, "Being the shortest day, tis the yeares midnight." When the Gregorian calendar reforms were instituted in the seventeenth-century, Lucy's day shifted backward by eleven days, to December 13.

The combination of Lucy's name and the date of her feast were the seeds of great popularity in the far north. By a process of communal imagination, she became a kind of angel of the solstice and its returning light. Lucy Fires—bonfires with handfuls of incense thrown on—accompanied by flutes and trumpets, heralded her day. Children would scrawl the name "Lussi" on walls, with a simple drawing of a female figure to protect against the winter demons. And so Lucy came to wear a crown of light, to lighten the dark predawn hours of her day. For centuries, the youngest girl in Scandinavian families has impersonated the solstice sun with her crown of candles, going from room to room in her home to wake the family from their deep midwinter sleep.

As the time ticks down to Christmas, the nights become more and more charged. In some parts of central Europe, the nine or twelve nights before Christmas are almost as festive as the twelve afterwards. These are called the "Golden Nights," since special observances are held at night. One of these is the Rorate Mass in honor of the Virgin Mary, celebrated in homes in the hours before dawn. A picture of the Blessed Virgin is then carried in a torch and lantern-light procession from house to house.

At the last minute, as all time runs toward midnight on Christmas Eve, the atmosphere of electric anticipation is powerful. Time is running out. All time and all people wait for the crisis of Christmas Eve midnight.

## *Entering the Season*

**The Advent wreath**—The finest piece of liturgy for Advent is a rite that can be done on the dining room table. Gift shops and Christian bookstores sell Advent candles. Wreaths can be easily made from evergreen boughs and wire; permanent wreaths—circular four-candle holders—are available, too. *Keeping Advent and Christmastime* (Liturgy Training Press, 2002), or *The Advent Wreath: A Light in the Darkness*, by Debbie Trafton O'Neal (Augsburg Fortress Publishers, 1989) are good guides to simple family observations centered on the wreath.

**Advent calendars**—A tradition from Germany, the Advent calendar is a scene, often of a village in winter, with doors and windows that open to reveal holiday images. The doors are numbered for the twenty-four days of December leading to Christmas, so that one door can be opened on each day of the month. These are effective icons for entering the experience of holy waiting. *Christmas in the Old Town Square*, illustrated by Phillipe Fix (Dutton Books, 1997), is a classic calendar.

**Flowers**—A number of legends talk about flowers that bloom wondrously at Christmastime, like England's famous Glastonbury thorn. Winter flowers symbolize the eruption into worldly time of God's cycles. You can create a symbol of this truth by planting paperwhite bulbs in gravel and forcing blooms by Christmas Day.

**"Guard of the Heart"**—As Father Thomas Keating writes, guard of the heart "is the practice of releasing upsetting emotions into the present moment. This can be done in one of three ways: doing what you are actually doing, turning your attention to some other occupation, or giving the feeling to Christ." This discipline is the inner equivalent of the old Advent customs of purification and protection.

## MUSIC

There is a lot of liturgical music for Advent, much is readily available due to the current popularity of medieval chant. One of the most plaintively lovely examples is from the women of Anonymous 4 on their CD, *A Star in the East: Medieval Hungarian Christmas Music* (Harmonia Mundi).

## READING

The best reading for Advent is *An Advent Sourcebook,* edited by Thomas J. O'Gorman (Liturgy Training Publications). This wealth of readings for Advent from many perspectives and all Christian eras explores an amazing number of the facets of the season—mystical, liturgical, historical, even political. Living with this book will help you become intimately familiar with the season.

Young Christmas Carolers, 1924. *Advent transforms the night-wanderers of autumn.*

WINTER

# WINTER

This is the night of mysteries for which we wait the whole year, the season of hidden light. This is when we come to the still point of the turning world, the time in the Year of the Lord when we tune our souls to adventure for the journey through midwinter darkness. We are given old patterns to follow, of revelry, prayer, and ritual; old rhythms of twelve holy nights and days worked out over many centuries by peasants, priests, and princes to accompany the great thing that is happening around us. This is the time of the radiant darkness, for the sun at midnight, that answers the terrible, practical noonday light of the mundane world.

The full Christmas season takes us from the end of November to the beginning of February. It is the swinging hinge of the year, the point at which one drama ends and the next begins.

*The Nativity*, Russian School, 16th century. *The Nativity, like the Resurrection, happens in a cave: a spark of eternity in the womb of the earth.*

# 5

# December 24

## CHRISTMAS EVE

*Far beneath the movement*

*of this silent cataclysm, Mary slept*

*in the infinite tranquility of God,*

*and God was a child curled up*

*who slept in her and her veins were flooded*

*with His wisdom which is night,*

*which is starlight,*

*which is silence.*

*And her whole being*

*was embraced in Him*

*whom she embraced*

*and they became*

*tremendous silence.*

—Thomas Merton


*When peaceful silence lay over all,*

*and the night had run half of her swift course,*

*your all-powerful word, O Lord, leapt down from heaven,*

*from the royal throne.*

—Wisdom 18: 14, 15

*Never we know but in sleet and in snow,*
*The place where the great fires are,*
*That the midst of the earth is a raging mirth,*
*And the heart of the earth a star.*

—G. K. Chesterton,
"A Child of the Snows"

## The Experience

Near the top of our tree we hang a small ornament that I picked up in a convenience store a few years ago. It's a plastic house, maybe three inches tall; it's a frame house, three stories, with a round conical tower on one side. You see a lot of houses like it in older American cities and towns. Prosperous middle-class people built them a hundred, a hundred-and-fifty years ago.

The ornament cost two or three dollars. It was probably pressed from a mold in southeast Asia, a mold that a novelty company might once have used for a toy village. But spray-painted a tarnished gold, hanging among the dark green branches in the glow from the colored lights, it is clearly not an ordinary house. Its windows hold a significant darkness.

There are different kinds of darkness, the same way that soil can be different kinds of black. Tear out a chunk of Midwestern corn-belt dirt; it is black like chocolate cake, an extravagant, rich black, the kind of dirt that small children want to eat. Then there's the dirt from other places, no-color grayish, sandy, clayey.

Darkness is like that. There's a kind of darkness that's just what happens when the lights go off. And then there's a dark that's a color in itself, a darkness that holds a lot inside, like that rich black dirt, a living dark that has velvety depth and goes back a long way. That's the kind of dark that is captured inside the little house by the simple trick of spray-painting it gold. What's inside the house? A big thing in a small space. "Eternity in a little, day in night, summer in winter." Christmas.

A tarnished gold strand leads back into the dark, a thread of memory from early childhood connecting you to all the Christmases that have come before: It is nighttime, and you are going up a walk to a big old house, with tall people alongside. Snow is falling, and you know that something is going to happen. But what? The familiar house becomes a strange labyrinth, where each room has a particular mood, like small theaters. It is an adventure just to go sit on a bed among a pile of coats, to smell the cold wool, look at the fall of light from the hallway and listen to the voices and music from downstairs. You rub a hole in the frost ferns on a window and gaze out at the snowy dark.

What is coming? What have we all gathered to wait for?

Christmas is a ritual—not just the part that happens in church, but what happens in our homes and lives in general. When we create an opening (symbolized by all the activity surrounding Christmas Eve) in the abstract, mechanical world of time, the real world that is going on all around us can come in. At midnight on Christmas Eve, Christ is born. For an instant the world stops and eternity intersects time.

There is a way known in Christian spirituality as the *via negativa*—the way of emptiness, or holy darkness. The old spiritual writers described it as "opposite the senses," by which they meant the distractions of the world. The *via negativa* is very much like traditions from India that call for emptying the mind. The Christian tradition has a distinctive emphasis, though, and that emphasis is love. The mystery that waits in the darkness, the timeless moment that Christmas midnight represents, is somehow love. We've been walking toward this moment since Michaelmas, or at least since Advent started.

This is a notable difference from the fear and trembling inspired by the great and terrible Oz; the Thunderers, Zeus and Odin; or even the Old Testament Yahweh. It is not like the Void in Eastern traditions or the impersonal lightning flash of *satori*. These are aspects of the divine, but not the one we approach on Christmas Eve.

People sometimes cry as they sing "Silent Night" at the end of a Christmas Eve service. Their five-year-old selves, the little mystics that live inside them, stir to life again and tear away the cobwebs that have shrouded their hearts over the past year.

Christmas Eve shows what all the sacred times of the Church Year are like when they come alive and are genuinely experienced. And since sacred times are any time when God slips into our lives, Christmas Eve is a dramatization of the possibility in any moment. It is the zero point of the spiritual year, the place where the great spiral that the sun traces in the sky winds down until it comes to the point where there is no time, where the day and the year end and begin, the place where we end and begin.

It occurs to me that something ought to be said here about a human problem with Christmas. When people write enthusiastically about timeless moments and spiritual experiences, it can actually have the effect of shutting their readers down. Many people come to Christmas each year wanting that great experience, yet never finding it. Because Christmas is the one point of sacred time that is also a part of our popular culture, it tends to backfire. What if the great moment goes by and we're tired or drunk or arguing with our spouse, or loaded with worry, sadness, or fear? What if the heart of the night doesn't open for us? What if all we hear is the laughter of the hot little devils from parking-lot land, because now they have us for another tired year?

In a way, Christmas is valued disproportionately, because most people don't have a single other ritual of sacred time in the whole year to help them distribute and develop the meaning of Christmas. This is why a new familiarity with the Year of the Lord can help the hurt that more and more people apparently associate with Christmas.

Sacred times are not necessarily extraordinary fairy-tale moments or spectacular altered states of consciousness. They are not given only to special people; they are not unusual. You live them every moment, even right now as you read this book. The moments of Christ are the material out of which everybody's lives are made. "A people without history cannot be redeemed from time," T. S. Eliot wrote, "because history is a pattern of timeless moments." It is your history, made up of nothing but timeless moments, that redeems you from time.

In the same way, as you go through a holiday, sacred time happens whether you feel it or not. You bustle through your Christmas obligations, right up to and maybe past midnight. Rest assured that above you, under you, inside you, the moment of Christmas is happening. "[T]he movement of this silent cataclysm," as Thomas Merton says, goes on. Sometime in the holy night something new happens, "a thrill of hope, the weary world rejoices."

The chronological clock-tick of midnight on Christmas Eve will come and go many times in your life without being a big moment. There is a spiritual principle that the more you want the big moment, the less likely you are to have it. This causes a lot of frustration and disappointment among people trying to practice a spiritual life, and at Christmastime, this disappointment spreads through the general public. If you don't get your big payoff at Christmas, it can sour you on the possibility of meaning and transcendence in general.

To experience Christmas *at* Christmas is a grace, a phenomenon that human will cannot make happen. The miraculous event of Christmas night is something that happens outside of time. All that any person can do is to *observe* the moment, in both senses of the word—the way we talk about observing a holiday, and to observe as in "to watch." To honor and observe the event of Christmas night is to build a ring of quiet around it, treading softly and slowly. As Christmas Eve day grows dark, give Christmas midnight its due. Give it space. Don't try to actualize some notion of a perfect atmosphere. Make one effort toward listening, watching, and observing, and you will be rewarded in some way.

Christmas, after all, is living, multifaceted, many layered. Christmas is not, in the words of G. K. Chesterton, just a "Scandinavian festival of peace." It is also a moment of extreme crisis, as reflected in the gospel stories of King Herod and his soldiers, who massacre the male children of Bethlehem in the hope of eliminating Jesus. Herod represents the forces of darkness, like the gathering winter gloom that seems more powerful than the glimmer of Christmas starlight. Herod is very much alive in our world—you can read about his exploits any day, in any newspaper. Chesterton says we should imagine the cave-stable of Jesus' birth as an outlaw hideout or a hidden rebel camp, the bells of Christmas night as distant cannons of a liberating army that are a signal for the resistance to rise up and cut the power lines and blow the rails. Christmas is a crisis, but at this darkest hour of the darkest night, the tide begins to turn.

Christmas Eve has a kind of suspense. The Son of Man comes like a thief in the night—and so does Santa Claus. Christmas Eve is when everything hangs in the balance for Ebenezer Scrooge, the night he sees ghosts and faces his own death. It is a last-minute impossible rescue from certain darkness. This is another theological truth that children know. "But in thy dark streets shineth the everlasting light. The hopes and fears of all the years are met in thee tonight." It translates here below as profound peace. Something enormous is going on, but it means us and our loved ones very clearly. It is just downstairs, by the tree, by the fire, just outside your door, in the sweet starlit darkness.

## *The Story*

We're frequently reminded that Christmas is not as important an event as Easter, and this is true theologically. But Christmas has grown as both a feast and in its effect on the human heart. Easter was charged with meaning from the beginning; Christmas has attained greater meaning with the passage of centuries.

Much of the power of Christmas results from its place in the year. The general consensus of historians is that Church authorities ordained the celebration of the Messiah's birth to coincide with an official Roman state holiday of the cult of Sol Invictus, the unconquered sun, at the time of the winter solstice. There was no thread of historical connection (as there was between Easter and Jesus' death) with the actual date of Jesus' birth.

THE HEARTH, WHERE WORLDS MEET, IS THE PLACE TO WAIT FOR CHRISTMAS EVE.

It turned out to be one of the Church's great strokes of inspiration for incorporating human traditions. During the third and fourth centuries, the attitude toward paganism was shifting. Christianity began to explain itself in language and symbols adapted from the mystery religions, whose traditions tapped into the same spiritual yearnings as Christianity. Christian writers found that images from classical mythology, such as the journey of Helios (the sun god) across the sky, resonated with the Christ story.

When the Church was a small and persecuted cult, it had much to fear in the state religion of Rome. The paganism of that era was not a happy religion of folk dancing in the greenwood; it was an integral part of the mechanics of a huge empire that was growing more inflated, garish, cruel, and corrupt at precisely the time the Church was developing. It identified divinity with power and used religion to keep order among its subjects. The gods of Rome had long since ceased to be spiritually or imaginatively alive.

It was only in the world of late antiquity that the Church began to open to the imaginative heritage of paganism. (This had a price: as the Church made its peace with the state, it became the state.) The Church had survived and grown and had become relatively tolerated (although there was one more spasm of disastrous persecution still ahead). As its Jewish roots receded farther into the past and the Church found its footing in the Roman world, Christianity took another step in assimilating images and patterns from the cosmopolitan Mediterranean culture that was now its home. Setting Christmas at the winter solstice was part of this process.

Over time the effect would be dramatic. Christmas on December 25 is a milestone in the absorption of Christianity into Western culture and Western culture into Christianity. Where Easter stretched one hand back to the Jewish matrix, Christmas reached the other arm out to the world. It is no coincidence that the solstitial Christmas was created at the same moment that Christianity became officially tolerated by the Empire and only a few years before it became the state religion.

Among the first traditions that Christmas absorbed were the Roman Saturnalia and the Kalendae of January. The Saturnalia lasted from December 17 through 24. Romans decked their homes with greenery, lit fires and candles, exchanged gifts, and played games that mimicked the reversal of established order. The New Year festival of the Kalendae continued the merriment in the first few days of January.

As the Church moved north into Europe, Christmas was a bridge to native peoples; everyone could recognize something in it. From prehistory, the northerners had acknowledged something enormous at the midwinter rebirth of the sun. Many of the chambered tombs and stone circles of northern Europe are oriented to the midwinter sunrise or sunset. Early medieval chroniclers and some of the early collections of legendary stories from these lands refer to a major midwinter feast. Wherever it went, Christmas carried an unspoken message to the heart. For the Saxons and Gaels, Allemani and Visigoths, the mystery of the winter woods now led to a radiant child and his mother. The old terrors of the forest, the hags and trolls and specters, became part of a holy pantomime with love at its center. The spread and growth of Christmas was a continuation of the Incarnation, the process of God entering the world.

The peoples of northern Europe had no written language, so we know very little about their customs and beliefs. But it can be assumed that many of the earliest Christmas traditions were adaptations of earlier pagan practices. The widespread idea that a period of days at the new year stood outside time and that the world then returned to the timeless state before creation, without boundaries between the spirit world and the human world, was probably part of these traditions. There was no plowing or harvesting to be done; flocks were down from their summer pastures. Meat from butchered animals had been smoked and salted for the winter and was ready to eat. It was a season of enforced leisure, a time for feasting, games, and decking the halls with greenery. The Night Wanderers were out, those fearful beings that gradually transformed into benevolent, if eerie, gift bringers. Their human counterparts, troupes of men and boys disguised as animals or spirits, probably went from homestead to homestead, performing, riddling, singing, or begging. Fields, orchards, and animals would be blessed and magically protected.

The hearth fire, then as now, had both a spiritual and symbolic importance. It is the sun within the home, the center and source of life and light. Sometimes the hearth is perceived as a connection between the home and the divine or spirit world. It is often associated with the presence of ancestors and guardian spirits. That Santa Claus enters and exits via the fireplace is an echo of these beliefs.

The early Christian missionaries brought Christmas to Europe, yet some parts of eastern Europe were not officially Christian until the turn of the first millennium. Ireland may have been one of the first; St. Patrick introduced Christmas there in the fifth century.

The early Middle Ages to the seventeenth century were the high point of Christmas as a religious and popular holiday. This was when most of the Christmas traditions were fully established: masquing and mumming, wassailing, the boar's head, gift giving, carols, midnight masses. With the Protestant Reformation of the sixteenth century and the Puritan Revolution in England in the seventeenth century, Christmas went into a long decline in non-Catholic Europe (though affection for the season stayed strong in Lutheran Germany). It was banned by Oliver Cromwell's Puritan government in England. It returned with the restoration of the monarchy. As a festival of the whole culture, though, it did not recover, and became a grab bag of half-remembered customs.

In the early nineteenth century, with increasing industrialization and the mass migration

SANTA CLAUS, BY WILLIAM BEARD (1824-1900). *AT MIDNIGHT ON CHRISTMAS EVE, ETERNITY ENTERS TIME, SOMETIMES IN DISGUISE.*

from agricultural communities to the cities, Christmas in Britain (except as a church service) seemed on its way to extinction. Its revival was due partly to urban middle-class families, who, with the inspiration of writers like Charles Dickens, rediscovered the old holiday. It was also inspired by the Romantic movement in the arts, which valued the imaginative worlds of popular culture, tradition, and folklore. The idea that common people had their own rich culture was revolutionary. The Grimm brothers' fairy tales were a typical product of this period. The revolutionary political spirit of the era energized the rediscovery of Christmas and other old holidays, since these offered an alternative to both aristocratic power and the remorseless tidal wave of capitalist industrialization.

In the United States, strangely enough, there was more of an unbroken link with old Christmas. While the northeast had initially been colonized by Puritan refugees from England (whose cultural influence was strong enough to keep Christmas from being recognized as a public holiday in Massachusetts until the late nineteenth century), the southern seaboard colonies were dominated by Royalist, High Church cavaliers—the political opponents of the Puritans and founders of the plantation economy—and Christmas flourished among them.

The real cradle of the popular American Christmas, however, was in the middle colonies of Maryland and Pennsylvania and on into the Ohio Valley. There it was nurtured by Irish, German, and eastern-European immigrants of the early nineteenth century. As their neighbors learned their beautiful Christmas traditions, the festival infiltrated the culture of America until it became universal.

Christmas Eve is the heart of the Christmas season, and midnight is the heart of Christmas Eve. This is traditionally the moment of Jesus' birth, the precise turning point between two years, two days, two seasons, two stages of human history. In fourth-century Rome, when December 24 was actually the solstice, Christmas Eve midnight was the exact moment at which the days began to lengthen. In some ancient mystery religions, the solstice midnight was the moment of initiation into divine life. In the language of Christian legend, the gates of paradise open at this moment, so that anyone dying then enters Heaven immediately. Children born on Christmas night have the power to see spirits. Animals, both domestic and wild, have the power of speech at that hour. Magical lights twinkle at the bottoms of caverns, mines, and wells. Evil spirits are rendered powerless, and the supernatural gift givers enter the household. Christmas Eve is the still point of the turning world. The drama of the year is resolved, and the next and greater cycle begins.

## *Entering the Season*

**Christmas Eve service**—Don't be shy. Even if you attend church at no other time of the year, you're still welcome. This is the rite of the season and, along with Easter Vigil, the most magical of the Church Year.

**Midnight**—Go out for a walk. You may be surprised at the quality of the silence.

**Santa Claus**—Santa (in works of varying levels of scholarship) has been interpreted as everything from a pagan deity to the deliberate creation of some prosperous New Yorkers desperate to protect their property values. However he came to be, Santa Claus is an icon of the love of God, with an icon's potential to be a window into the thrill and mystery of imaginative truth. Bring him alive—reverently, gently, fully alive—for your kids, and you and they will never regret it.

## MUSIC

Some of the best music for Christmas Eve comes out of the English choral tradition. Recordings of English choirs, often made in cathedrals, churches, and chapels, may not always meet audiophile standards, but the sound of soft human voices against old stone is one of the sweet fruits of Western liturgical art. The standards include: John Rutter, *Christmas Night* (Collegium CD106, 1993); David Willcocks, conductor, *Noel: Christmas at King's* (Polygram Records CD444848, 1995); King's College Choir, *A Festival of Nine Lessons and Carols* (Angel Classics CD73693, 1999); and Benjamin Britten, *A Ceremony of Carols,* David Willcocks, conductor (EMI Classics Import CD 764653, 2001).

## READING

Charles Dickens's *A Christmas Carol in Verse, Being a Ghost Story of Christmas* is a dream adventure, a death and rebirth *inside this very night.* It's been popular since 1843 for good reason, as the London gloom Dickens sets against all the interior light and warmth is near the heart of things at this time of year. Read it carefully. Notice there is no snow and no Christmas tree. Notice how economically and politically pointed is Jacob Marley's critique of Scrooge, who doesn't produce anything but rather is part of the New Economy, 1840s-style. Most of all, notice how love begins its work in the heart of the cold and dark.

C. Clement Moore's "A Visit from St. Nicholas" (*'Twas the Night before Christmas, or An Account of a Visit from St. Nicholas,* Candlewick Press, 2002) concerns a nineteenth-century American bourgeois who has a close encounter on Christmas Eve. The power here has to do with waking up in the middle of a winter night, going downstairs, and entering a dream.

Susan Hill's *Can It Be True?* (Viking Press, 1988) with illustrations by Angela Barrett is a beautiful picture book with the feel of an English folk song. A transformation happens wordlessly across the icy countryside as the great news travels through all the levels of creation.

*Twelfth Night at Haddon Hall, Derbyshire, 16th century. Impersonating mystery; Twelve Days to act out the miraculous meaning of Christmas.*

# 6

# JANUARY 5

## TWELFTH NIGHT
## (THREE KINGS' NIGHT)

# JANUARY 6

## THE FEAST OF THE EPIPHANY

*Epiphany: (proto Indo-European)* bhan-yo, *"to shine";*

*(Greek)* phainein, *"to bring to light," to "cause to appear," "to show . . ."*

*He shall be a light to enlighten the nations . . .*

—The Song of Simeon, Luke 2:32

*Why not be totally changed into fire?*

—Abbot Joseph of Egypt

*Christ is never unaccompanied by water.*

—Bishop Tertullian

*Today the whole universe is refreshed by mystical streams.*

—Orthodox Liturgy for Epiphany

## The Experience

Twelve is completeness—twelve apostles, twelve months to the year, twelve hours of day, twelve houses of the zodiac; twelve to a dozen, twelve inches to the foot, twelve jurors in the box. The Christmas season offers a complete festive circle of twelve days that dance around the axis of the year. By and large, we don't accept the offer.

Christmas is not a day, it's a season. The observance of Christmas Day is unfinished and unbalanced without the twelve holy days and nights that follow. The calendar of commerce exalts the preparation for Christmas, then recognizes no time for letting Christmas develop naturally afterward. This creates a real psychic rupture that is felt not just in our individual lives but in our social world. It is one reason why many people dislike Christmas. The joy and pleasure that greeted the reinvigorated Christmas of the nineteenth century has been overstimulated, overdosed, overwhelmed.

Certainly there was materialism in the nineteenth-century Christmas, close enough to its heart so that a secular historian can make a convincing case that middle-class prosperity was its true source. The enormous energy of triumphant capitalism was a powerful engine for popularizing Christmas; but after commerce inflated the holiday, it began to cannibalize it.

To observe even a part of the real Christmas season—that is, *after* Christmas Day—is to draw a line in the sand against the commercial Christmas calendar, and it is not an arbitrary line. There is a natural spiritual rhythm to the development of the Christmas holy days. Ideally, the burst of energy at Christmas works its way through the spirit over the following days until it's integrated into daily life. Instead, the intense inflation of excitement that now, under commercial pressure, ends on Christmas Day, violates and blocks this flow. To return to the mundane, unfestive world too quickly after Christmas is like going swimming too soon after you eat—you get psychic cramps. (I should confess here that the author is not immune. You are reading the words of a person who begins to get excited about Christmas at the end of August; a person who *likes* walking around malls listening to Christmas carols.)

The twelve days are the fullness of Christmas. They are the time required to bring the event that takes place at midnight on Christmas Eve to its full development. All the intricate gaming and dancing and masquing of medieval and Renaissance Europe was a way to act out that process. To eliminate these observances creates, as I've said, a rupture. The effect is exacerbated as the commercial pre-Christmas season grows longer and more agitated. The great roaring engine of the Christmas commerce complex plows into the icy dark heart of winter on December 26, and grinds to a sudden shocking halt.

There is no chance, of course, that the Western world will shut down between December 25 and January 6, and I'm not suggesting that we use up our vacation days in midwinter. But we must make some respectful gesture to leisure in the time immediately after Christmas Day, even if it is only one day. If we want to take the ritual year more seriously, we must begin with the time after Christmas.

We feel something more elemental during the twelve days than we do at Easter-tide. Midwinter is in our blood and dreams, in the rhythm of earth and sun. Historians describe the gradual accumulation of Christian holy days immediately following Christmas—St. Stephen, the Holy Innocents, St. John the Evangelist, and others—as something that just sort of happened. But the twelve days are no accident. Many archaic calendars have a holy period of about twelve days at the new year, a period added on to the twelve lunar months to equal the full solar cycle. These traditions arise out of a mismatch in length between the lunar and solar years.

This arrangement became an administrative problem for the Roman Empire as it tried to coordinate the solar Julian calendar with the lunar calendars of its provinces in the east. While the Romans could roughly match the months in the two systems, the four cardinal points of the solar year—the two equinoxes and solstices—still fell on different dates. By the time of the first century, the calendar date of the winter solstice in Egypt and Palestine was eleven to twelve days later than the date in Rome. As a result, the Incarnation came to be celebrated on different days in different parts of the Empire. The Western Church, in its desire to be universal, eventually took them both—one became Christmas, one Epiphany—with a resulting twelve days in between.

Over time this hiatus became invested with specific Christian meaning. The Church gradually filled these days with saints, some connected to the birth narratives in the Gospels (Holy Innocents' Day, December 28, in honor of the infants slaughtered by Herod; St. John the Evangelist, "the Beloved," December 27; St. Stephen, the first Christian martyr, December 26; the Holy Family, December 31; the Virgin Mary, January 1). In 567, the Council of Tours declared the twelve days between Christmas and Epiphany to be one unified festal cycle.

In the Christian calendar, the season flowers from the infinitesimal crack in time on

Christmas Eve. The light, love, and energy that arc from eternity to mundane time take shape as a miniature model of all time—the twelve days.

A world that could have twelve days of Christmas would be very different from our own. It would be a world run by the agricultural and pastoral calendar, where at midwinter there is a time of leisure. There is a grace and spaciousness in the idea of the twelve days, a lavish spending of time. To set aside twelve days of potentially productive time to celebrate a holiday would be a sacrifice. What God gives back are rest and pleasure.

There's something magical and antiquarian about the phrase, "the Twelve Days of Christmas." It suggests a missing fullness. It calls up phantasmagorical images of Old Christmas—theatrical enactments of midwinter mystery; Christmas masques in the court of the Stuart kings with round dances, gilded masks, spangled costumes, and suns and moons dangling from roof beams. Sometimes, late on a winter night when the house is quiet, looking into the quiet shining and strange splendor of a Christmas tree can take us there.

Further back and stranger still, there are the kings—wise men from the East, their robes glittering with signs—and their rich and cryptic gifts. The kings are magi, magicians who have knowledge of the mysteries of God. They are ambassadors from the world of mysticism and gnosis.

Not for nothing is Peter, the man whom Jesus nicknamed "the Rock" (who is consistently shown in all the Gospels as just not understanding what Jesus is trying to say), the founder of the Western Christian tradition. The Rock is the original square, the apostle to the rectilinear Romans and the roughneck northern barbarians they ruled over. So it's not surprising that Western Christendom has historically downplayed systems for gaining conscious knowledge of God. In fact, the Western Church does understand the art and science of the spiritual life: It is called "ascetical theology." It is still practiced in monastic communities and expressed in classic works of the devotional and contemplative life by Clement of Alexandria, St. Bonaventure, St. Bernard of Clairvaux, John of the Cross, and Theresa of Avila, as well as in lesser-known works, such as the *Showings* of Julian of Norwich, the anonymous *Cloud of Unknowing*, and the writing of Hildegard of Bingen, Meister Eckhart, and Jean-Pierre de Caussade.

However, in the eastern half of the Roman sphere—the vast arc from Greece to Egypt—there were the wise men, philosophers, poets, dramatists, and astrologers who were the heirs of Osiris, Solomon, Plato, Zoroaster, Orpheus, and Hermes Trismegistus. A priest I know

*ADORATION OF THE MAGI. RELIEF FROM RASM-EL-GANAFEZ, DAMASCUS. AT EPIPHANY, THE ANCIENT WORLD'S WISDOM IS INVITED TO BETHLEHEM.*

once said, "You've got to remember, at the beginning, Christianity was an *Eastern* religion." The original tongue of the Church was Greek, the subtle universal language of the Eastern Empire. John, the mystical gospel writer and "beloved apostle," lived and died in Asia Minor; Doubting Thomas (of the gnostic gospel) was in India, according to tradition. Almost all of St. Paul's work was in that oriental crescent. Jesus grew to manhood four miles from a bustling gentile-Greek metropolis called Sepphoris. The Eastern Church, which grew from this world, is the church of the art of prayer and the beauty of God.

This was the world of the three magi.

*Epiphany* comes from the Greek, meaning "to shine light upon, to show or to make visible." It is the name for the feast commemorating the manifestation of Christ to the nations. This is a way of saying that Christianity is a universal religion, not in the sense that all humanity will or even should become formally Christian, but that Christian truth is the truth in all human experience—a gathering of wisdom to a focal point. So in the gospel story of the magi, the representatives of wisdom come to Bethlehem to acknowledge the dawn of a new era.

The Feast of the Epiphany seems to have come from Egypt as a commemoration of Jesus' baptism in the Jordan River, his anointing by John, and his illumination by the Holy Spirit. For centuries, this was, in effect, Christmas, since many early Christians placed more emphasis on Jesus' baptism rather than his conception or birth. Epiphany is associated with the poetry of light and water. In Greek Orthodoxy, baptism is *pho tizesthai* (to illuminate), rather than *bap tizesthai* (to wash). At baptism, each person is illuminated with the light of Christ, just as Jesus was illuminated by the Holy Spirit on the banks of the Jordan. St. Proclus, the Patriarch of Constantinople, says, "Christ manifested Himself to the world; He filled it with light and joy; He sanctified the waters and diffused His light in the souls of men." Epiphany, as Christmas would also be, is the feast of lights.

Water is a symbol of birth and transformation. When Jesus is submerged in the water of that muddy Middle Eastern stream, water itself is sanctified and becomes the universal channel of the spirit, flowing from that spot into all the waters of the world and throughout humanity.

The Egyptian Christians took great delight in the Epiphany. There is a paradisal atmosphere in the descriptions of the festivities. At Alexandria and on the Nile, parties went out on illuminated boats at night, feasting and bathing, pouring scented oil on the waters. They collected the waters of that night for blessing their boats throughout the year. The tenth-century Egyptian historian Al-Massoudi says it was "the night of most pleasure" in Egypt. He describes gold and silver musical instruments, food and drink, jewelry and festive dress. Set into the floors of the Coptic churches were special pools for festive bathing on Epiphany.

Poetically, the liturgy of Epiphany uses the image of water the same way Jesus does in the Gospel of John, when he talks to the Samaritan woman at the well about the "living water," an image of the new life he offers. Epiphany enriches the imagery by weaving in the story of Jesus' first miracle, turning water into wine. The story of the wedding at Cana unfolds the symbol of water one turn further. Wine was a symbol of spiritual water. The Hebrew word for "living water" also means "flowing water." Wine has its own interior flow or life. Jesus is accused by his enemies of being a "glutton and a wine-bibber"; "the Son of Man came eating and drinking," he says of himself. Again and again in the Gospels, we relax at table with Jesus and his disciples and what seem to be dozens of other people—rich and poor, friends and strangers—buzzing around. His last activity before his death was a dinner party. At that Last Supper, he looks with infinite sadness at his wine and tells his friends that he won't be sharing the cup with them anymore, not until they gather again in the Kingdom of Heaven.

Light, water, wine: we walk the ground of the ancient Near East, dusty, thirsty, footsore travelers. We are invited to leave this arid world and jump into a river.

We've traveled a long way, from shopping malls to Elizabethan London to Egypt. The shoppers shop; the revelers dance; the magi come to the stable; Jesus comes to the river, the huge sun overhead. In cool clay jars, water turns to wine. Like all the holy days, the twelve days from Christmas to the Feast of the Epiphany open up paths, unlocking level after level of meaning. These days, the path leads to an abandoned settlement, an archeological dig. Yet treasures lie below the surface: when we dig down, there are living springs.

## The Story

Epiphany is older than Christmas. The three kings, as envoys from the ancient Orient, are good guides into its origins. Like the kings, Epiphany comes with trappings of far-off and mysterious lands, in particular, first-century Egypt, where the remains of the old pharaonic culture became the distinctive Coptic Christian civilization.

Epiphany traditionally celebrates three events: the arrival of the magi in Bethlehem, the baptism of Jesus in the Jordan, and Jesus' first miracle at the wedding in Cana. (In the 1950s, the Roman Catholic Church moved the commemoration of the baptism one week past Epiphany Sunday to prevent its eclipse by the popular magi.) In the Eastern Church, January 6 is, as the Episcopal *Lesser Feasts and Fasts* calls it, "the primary feast of the Incarnation"—Christmas. For a long time in the early Christian period, however, it had nothing to do with Jesus' birth.

As we've mentioned, there have been differing opinions as to when exactly God became incarnate in Jesus. Modern Christians take for granted that God was fully present in the embryonic Jesus of Nazareth. Many early Christians, though, felt that it was only at his baptism that God became fully present in Jesus. This idea implies a more subtle mingling of the divine and human in Jesus. Rather than being divine from birth (or conception), Jesus becomes divine when he is well into adulthood. It implies a decision on the part of the human Jesus—that he sought the birth of God in himself. It also implies spiritual growth, in radical contrast to the static and supernatural Savior that most Christians recognize.

This idea came to be known as *adoptionism*, and was eventually classified as heresy. Still, something of the idea persists in the significance accorded to Jesus' baptism as more than a pro forma courtesy that Jesus accepted from John the Baptist. Only two of the Gospels contain accounts of the Annunciation or the Nativity, but all four prominently feature his baptism near or at the start of the story. The ecstatic language in the gospel accounts and in the Eastern liturgies show that something important happened to Jesus at his baptism—the archetype of what happens to his followers at their baptisms.

During Epiphany, the imagery of baptism is explored. In Eastern Orthodox liturgy, ponds, streams, rivers, lakes, and oceans are blessed in open-air services. Early theologians describe how the masculine element of the Holy Spirit, symbolized by the fire of a candle, and the feminine element of baptismal water give birth to the newly initiated Christian. After Easter Eve, the Eve of Epiphany was long considered the best moment for baptism. The early Church fathers spoke of baptism as illumination, and of Epiphany as the Feast of Lights or the Day of Illumination.

Epiphany also developed images from contemporary traditions of the Mediterranean world. January 6, the date of the solstice in Eastern calendars, was observed as the start of the new year. Around the time of Jesus, there was a new-year rite in the Egyptian city of Alexandria, that polyglot capital of Jewish, Greek, pharaonic, and Christian ideas. It seems to have been a festival of one of the mystery religions, using symbols from the cult of Isis. On January 5, devotees kept vigil all night long. At cockcrow, a statue of the goddess was brought from an underground chamber and carried seven times around the temple to the accompaniment of flutes, kettledrums, and chants, the worshippers crying, "At this hour the virgin has given birth!"

Also in Egypt and the eastern Mediterranean were rituals that involved the sanctification or transformation of water, sometimes expressed as water turning into wine. There are several references in classical literature to festivals of Dionysus in which water was believed to change into wine, at least one of which was on January 5.

As happened with other parts of the calendar, the Church Year would revive and transform the prehistoric sense of time. As we've seen, by the time of the empire, much of the old sacred perception of the annual cycles had faded in the daylight of the Roman administrative-commercial mind. The Jewish religion, too, had rejected the cyclical time of the agricultural religions in favor of the long road from Eden to Apocalypse. But in the Christian calendar, that twelve-day lag between the two calendars of the empire became again a sacred period.

The Twelve Days of Christmas really took on a body as the Church grew in northern Europe. Here, as in so many places, the liturgy was filled out by the artistry of the people and their traditions. Many of these showed the sense of peril and crisis at this time of the year. The list of folk customs celebrated in the Twelve Days of Christmas has filled volumes. In general, it was a time of festivity, games, song, and dance, the pouring out of wealth, generosity, entertainments, feasting, and the year's most intense period of mumming and guising. As soon as systematic record keeping began in western Europe in the early Middle Ages, we find accounts of festivities in the great strongholds, palaces, and manor houses. From the fourth to the eleventh centuries, there are also records of Church authorities regularly denouncing indigenous midwinter revelry, in particular divination and mumming.

There is a powerful and striking consistency in the mood and atmosphere of new-year customs, from Mesopotamia to Scandinavia. In the earliest human imagination, this holy period was a return to the golden age of hilarious freedom before the laws of time, nature, history, cause and effect came into play. Lords of Misrule and Masters of Revels were appointed to direct the twelve days and nights. Beggars became kings and kings became fools. The selection of mock kings by drawing lots, or by finding a coin or a bean baked in a cake, is one of the great European pastimes at Twelfth Night, and almost certainly prehistoric.

It was also the season of masks. Called "disguising" or "guising," "mumming" and "masquing," men and women with the heads of gorgeous birds and monsters, peacocks and dragons, angels and wild men would dance in the courts of Elizabeth Tudor and James Stuart. Over the years these became elaborate dramas, lavish and outlandish spectacles filled with strange hermetic symbols.

Something similar happened in the village streets. Groups of mummers appeared in the wildest costumes that old trunks in farmhouses and cottages could provide. In later centuries, they enacted a strange drama in which a black knight kills St. George, and a doctor is brought on to bring him back to life. In Scotland, men wearing cowhides ran sunwise around houses to bless them. The skeleton horse, the Mari Llwyd, or gray mare, made her clacking appearance outside the door. To this day at Abbot's Bromley in the English Midlands, two teams of men carrying painted reindeer horns (carbon dated to the eleventh century) fight a mock battle—perhaps a battle between winter and summer.

Epiphany, of course, commemorates the magi who follow the star of Bethlehem to pay homage to Jesus at his birth. *Magi* is the Latin plural of *magus,* or magician. The original Greek word in the New Testament refers to practitioners of Eastern magical arts, such as astrology and dream interpretation. Early English translators of the Bible rendered it as "wise men."

The Greek historian Herodotus says that magi were priests of Zoroastrianism, the Persian religion. Later it was claimed that magi meant "lords" or "rulers." Because the Gospel of Matthew mentions the three gifts of gold, frankincense, and myrrh (said to symbolize kingship, divinity, and sacrifice), we have our beloved three kings, named Gaspar, Melchior, and Balthazar. (There are twelve in the Eastern Church.)

The Adoration of the Magi is one of the first images in Christian art, and in early relief sculptures they are indeed portrayed as Persian priests. They came to be associated with the prophecy from the Psalms that the kings of far, exotic lands would come to pay homage to the God of Israel.

Over time the idea developed that the magi symbolized all the races of humankind, so that one is depicted as white, one brown, and one black, and they are given different widely separated kingdoms. (The implication from the Gospels is that they all came from one country.) They are said to have later gone to evangelize the extreme east, in India.

Though in the gospel story the kings arrive soon after the birth of the Messiah, they came relatively late to their own holiday. Epiphany had been celebrated in the East for centuries before it was adopted by the Western Church. It was only then that the feast was associated with the kings.

The gospel story contains an echo of the split with Judaism, in that the gentiles recognize Christ while the Jewish authorities do not. But it also contains another meaning. What comes to Christ in the persons of the magi is the spiritual wisdom of the old Near-Eastern civilizations and, by extension, the spiritual wisdom of the world.

This points to another theme within the story of the kings. *Magic* has always had several different meanings. Most of the world's religions proscribe magic in the sense of spells, charms, fortune-telling, and as a means of self-aggrandizement or exerting power. But magic also refers to systems of symbol and ritual that teach deep knowledge of the workings of the spirit. Magic in this sense is the science of the spirit. It teaches how holiness works. Every religion has a body of wisdom like this, and it has nothing to do with superstition or the abuse of power. The Kabbalah of Judaism is one such magical system, and the rabbis who developed it were men of great sanctity. In this sense the wise kings really were magicians.

## *Entering the Season*

**Celebrating the full Christmas season**—Begin to shift your celebration's center of gravity from *before* to *after* December 25. Most importantly, take time off somewhere between Christmas Day and Epiphany, even if it's just a day for rest and re-creation.

*New Year's Eve*—This observance did not randomly fall into this period from some other tradition—it's the fulcrum of the twelve nights. Put it into the context of Christmastide. Play Christmas music. Light a fire. Go see a production of *A Christmas Carol.* Go caroling. Or sit quietly and recollect each month from the past year; then think ahead to the year to come. How would you like each one in the new year to be different—or perhaps the same?

*Twelfth Night*—Throw a party complete with Twelfth Night games. Card games, guessing games, word games, board games, silly games, drinking games, games of chance—Twelfth Night is a night of silly and trivial rules and roles, carefully observed. The twelve days are also a season of masks. Small skits, role-playing games, even a simple game of charades are all in the spirit of the season. Some other ideas:

- *Snap Dragon*—This Victorian after-dinner entertainment is atmospheric and slightly hair-raising, though quite safe. Put several handfuls of raisins in a large shallow dish. Heat some (cheap) brandy, pour it in the dish and set fire to it. The players pluck the raisins out. You won't get burned, but it's not for children or the easily panicked. Most impressive and dramatic with the lights out—the blue light dances across the bowl.

- *Kings by Lottery*—Choosing a mock king by lots is a tradition as old as Saturnalia. One way is to hide something—an uncooked bean, a coin etc.—in a cake. Whoever gets the slice with the token is King (or Queen) of Twelfth Night, and can order the other partiers to perform silly stunts.

**Eastern Orthodox blessing of water**—In many Eastern Orthodox churches, Epiphany features a beautiful rite of the blessing of water. Weather permitting, congregations gather at some nearby body of open water for a ritual that goes back to ancient Egypt and celebrates the streams of living water that Christ sets flowing at this time.

## MUSIC

Jean Ritchie, *Kentucky Christmas Old and New* (Green Hays Records CD, 1994).

Robin Williamson, *Winter's Turning* (Flying Fish Records CD, 1992).

The Chieftains, *The Bells of Dublin* (RCA, 1991).

The Christmas Revels, *Christmas Day in the Morning, To Drive the Dark Away, A Child's Christmas Revels,* and *A Victorian Revels.* These may be ordered through the Christmas Revels website at *http://revels.bizland.com/store/page1.html,* or through your local record store.

Maggie Sansone, *Sounds of the Season 1 & 2* (Maggie's Music, 1990); *Ancient Noels* (Maggie's Music, 1993); *A Scottish Christmas* (Maggie's Music, 1996).

## READING

Miles and John Hadfield, *The Twelve Days of Christmas* (Cassell, 1961). A readable, nicely illustrated work of popular scholarship that introduces us to the richness of the Twelve Days.

CELTIC CROSS, CLONMACNOISE, IRELAND. *THE CELTIC CHURCH, OF BRIGID AND PATRICK, HINTS AT A DIFFERENT WAY TO SEE HISTORY.*

# 7

# FEBRUARY 1

## THE FEAST OF ST. BRIGID OF IRELAND

# FEBRUARY 2

## THE PURIFICATION OF ST. MARY THE VIRGIN
## (THE PRESENTATION OF OUR LORD)
## CANDLEMAS

*Ich am of Irelonde,*

*and of the holy launde of Irelonde*

*Gode Sir, for sainte Charitee,*

*Pray come daunce with me,*

*In Irelonde.*

—Anonymous, medieval Ireland

*As these tapers burn with visible fire*

*and dispel the darkness of night,*

*so may our hearts with the help of thy grace*

*be enlightened by the invisible fire*

*of the splendor of the Holy Ghost.*

—Roman Catholic prayer for Candlemas

*A flock of birds settles*
*in a land where a woman dwells;*
*a green field abounds with noise*
*in which is a brook, swift, green, bright.*

—May Song, Ireland, fifteenth century

## The Experience

As residents of the upper Midwest of the United States know, winter never actually ends. It hangs on interminably, miserably, through almost half the year, like a neurotic house guest you invited for Christmas who won't leave, filling ashtrays, piling up dishes in the sink, and leaving dirty socks on the dining-room table. Even in May, winter is liable to pop back up like some gruesome jack-in-the-box.

We might choose February as the most bleak and mundane of months, the embodiment of T. S. Eliot's "waste sad time, before and after." A sad month, when Christmas magic is a distant memory, the first grim weeks of Lent loom, and Easter isn't even on the horizon. February is nowhere.

If we can hallow February we can hallow any time.

Yet even here the Year of the Lord gives meaning to meaningless time with symbols and rituals that teach us to look contemplatively below the surface bleakness. A little cluster of spiritual activity buzzes around the very beginning of February, two feasts that hallow this time of year, while the time of year illuminates the meaning of the feasts. Two great ladies enter the season now: St. Brigid, who watches over animals, "the high maid of Ireland," midwife of Christ, lady of the sacred fire, has her feast forty days after Christmas, followed the next day by one of the great feasts of Mary, the Mother of God.

Brigid, "the fiery arrow" (as her name means in Irish Gaelic), is both a Celtic goddess and the great Christian patroness of Ireland. As both goddess and saint, Brigid is a bridge between two phases of spiritual history. She stands for the process whereby paganism flowed into Christianity rather than being vanquished by it. She is one of the helpers of Christ who carried the Christian story deep into the heart and imagination of the native people of Ireland. Brigid is a *mid*wife, whose place is in the middle, helping something new out of something old.

Mary, as the *mediatrix* or mediator between the heavenly world and the human world, is a bridge, too. And Candlemas is a bridge between the end of the Christmas cycle and the beginning of spring.

The dogmatic masculine vision of Church history sees Christianity only at certain sharp points where it is most distinct from everything else. These holidays have to do with the feminine dynamics of flow and growth. They remind us that the pointed masculine vision often misses the point. Sacred history is living history, and living things grow from one stage to another. Thus, in lands like Ireland, you indeed end up with a distinctly different religious culture than you began with, but through a continuum of growth, metamorphosis, and resurrection. Though the Celtic monks were fiercely ascetic, there is a sense that the evangelization of the indigenous peoples was as much an organic development as a conversion. A flower is different from a seed, but they are part of the same process, and Brigid is its patroness.

Something like this happened with the Coptic Christians of Egypt, evangelized very early by Christians from Palestine. Just as in Egypt you can see the *ankh*—the pharaonic looped cross or "key of life"—side by side with the Christian cross in early Coptic architecture, so in Ireland the distinctive Celtic cross of St. Patrick—the cross within a circle—is an adaptation of a native sun symbol. These two styles of indigenous Christianity, Egyptian and Irish, also share a strong inclination toward monasticism and the contemplative life.

Celtic Christianity, of which Brigid is a representative, is a popular topic these days, though it is not well defined in many of the books written about it. In rite and doctrine, the Church in Ireland was not so different from Rome, but at the level of the common people, it was a very distinct world. The relatively peaceful transition here from paganism to Christianity allowed the growth of a unique religious culture marked by passion and creativity that adapted traditional artistic life to the Christian story. Fittingly, St. Brigid is a patroness of artisans.

The spiral pattern of the Year of the Lord is a feminine pattern that gets you from one thing to another without discontinuity. One of the oldest religious symbols, you can see the spiral carved in the stones of ancient British monuments. The Celtic cross is a flattened spiral—it goes outward and around at the same time. Brigid is the process through which hearts are converted by a natural movement toward God.

This vision of history never becomes the official version. Conventional scholarship tends to miss the way that people actually experience life because it depends on making distinctions, often arbitrary ones. As G. K. Chesterton says, "The great mass of men are poets, but for some reason I have never heard explained, it is only the minority of unpoetical people who get to write critical studies."

St. Brigid points to another kind of history. Brigid is hard to pin down. Her various life stories portray her as both a fifth-century Irish abbess and also somehow present at Jesus' birth. She looms large in the history of her land: the cathedral, convent, and monastery at Kildare that she is credited with founding had a documentable effect on Irish life. On the other hand, she may never have really existed. She is a figure of in-betweens, the feminine both/and instead of the masculine either/or. She lives in the connecting places between the sharp points. The women of the Hebrides who called Brigid into their homes on the eve of her feast were not inviting a historical personage, but a living presence.

Mary's holiday and Brigid's are not shattering interruptions or breakthroughs like Easter and Christmas. They are in the middle of a quiet process of transformation, a stage in the slow warming and enlivening of things. Brigid, they say in the Western Isles of Scotland, breathes life into the mouth of dead winter with a kiss, a beautiful metaphor for the real rhythm of a spiritual life.

These two feasts come when winter-locked nature begins to ease toward flow. In the many saints' wells of Britain and Ireland, ice was melting at this time. If you were watching one of them at midnight on the eve of Brigid's day, you might glimpse a magic or immortal fish. To see one of these supernatural salmon or trout meant that your prayers would be granted. In the spiritual life, this is the moment when the armor can begin to fall off. C. S. Lewis said that at one point in his conversion, he felt something unpleasantly like the trickling of ice water down his back, as if he were a melting snowman.

The warmth and love that the Irish feel for their saints may be due to the fact that when Christianity arrived, the people recognized a part of the Divine that they had known for a long time. The festival of St. Brigid was a lyrical, warm, and slightly eerie celebration of feminine power. Its atmosphere owed much to its pagan origins, but it was gentle and full of soft light, a festival of home and hearth, centered around inviting Brigid into the house from the kindly dark of the first mild nights.

This winter-spring feast of Brigid is a legacy from long-ago mothers, from the realm of mother-wit and mother night, of grannies by the fire; a woman's world of birthing babies and burying bodies in the ground. New Testament scholar John Dominic Crossan has speculated that the earliest oral sources of the Passion narratives—the story of Jesus' arrest, trial, suffering, and death—may have originated as a lament, created and sung by the women of the

Jesus movement. All over Europe and the Middle East, it was women who mourned the dead, who composed and sang the laments, who counted the losses and sufferings of the bitterly hard lives that most people lived—and still live. There is a powerful imaginative tendency to associate femaleness with the earth and with origins. In the mythology of temperate lands, the earth brings forth all living things and is also the dark womb that receives all humans at the end. The barrow mounds of the old European landscape are verdant swollen bellies of earth.

Candlemas, the year's first great feast of Mary, marks the full end of the process that began in late November with Advent. Like all of its predecessors in the Christmas cycle, Candlemas is a rite of light in darkness. At Candlemas we are over the worst. The single light of the Christmas star is spreading now. The entire congregation carries candles and the church is illuminated with the promise of the coming spring. Mild Mary of the blue mantle is present in the softening dark.

Historians can find no objective reason for the pairing of the feast days of Brigid and Mary, but there is a poetic and symbolic logic to it. To mix traditions, you might say that Brigid is an avatar of Mary, of divine tenderness. She's been called "the Mary of the Gaels." Together, the two are a celebration of woman, the feminine attributes of God and nature, at the time when harsh winter begins to yield, the lambs suckle, and the earth shows the first signs of life.

## The Story

Brigid is the "Mother Saint" of Ireland, credited, along with Patrick, with converting the Irish to Christianity. Unlike Patrick, there is no direct evidence that she ever existed. There is an Irish goddess of the same name, with some of the same characteristics as the saint. In fact, Brigid is one of the likelier examples of a pagan deity metamorphosing into a Christian legend with, perhaps, no intervening human being involved.

The earliest account of her life was written about 125 years after the supposed date of her death. There are a number of lives of St. Brigid from the early medieval centuries, varying widely in basic facts, and highly fantastic in much of their content. It should be said, though, that fantastic tales are told of other Celtic saints who certainly did exist; and in the sixth century *someone* founded the great convent and cathedral complex at Kildare that has always been associated with her name.

St. Brigid, engraving ca. 1810. *Brigid prayed that the Holy Family might have a "lake of beer."*

St. Brigid, as her persona developed over the Middle Ages, was a composite creation. We've seen a similar process at work with St. Lucy of Advent, a real Christian martyr who took on traits of northern female winter spirits. St. Nicholas made a similar, even longer, journey from Turkey to the Netherlands, where he, too, assumed qualities of supernatural beings already in residence.

As an individual, St. Brigid leaves fewer historical traces than Nicholas or even Lucy, though her effect on her native land is greater. But the gods or spirits that flit around Lucy and Nicholas are shadowy and hypothetical. With Brigid, the pagan goddess in question is much closer to the surface. We don't have to guess who the saint was joining forces with.

The pagan goddess and the Christian saint occupied the same landscape; they were natives, not immigrants like Nicholas or Lucy (who arrived in their northern homes when the population was already Christianized). According to her various biographies, St. Brigid was as much involved in the conversion of the Irish as her contemporary, Patrick. No wonder that Celtic goddess and Christian holy woman are fused so completely that it is impossible to separate them.

Brigid the goddess seems to have been particularly mild and benevolent for a Celtic deity. She was a goddess of learning, poetry, prophecy, healing, and metalworking. Brigid the saint was a patroness of students and founded a school of art that included metalwork and illumination. The most famous product of the school's scriptorium was the wondrous *Book of Kildare*, an illuminated gospels that was so gorgeously decorated that Giraldus Cambrensis, chronicler of King Arthur, wrote that it seemed to be "the work of angelic, and not human skill."

In the Irish imagination, St. Brigid (also lovingly known as "Bride") was transported back in time to be Mary's midwife and wet nurse to the infant Jesus. In the Western Isles of Scotland, when a midwife was called to a woman in labor, she would first stop at the threshold of the house, place her hands on the doorposts, and say,

*Bride, Bride, come in,*
*Thy welcome is truly made.*
*Give thou relief to the woman*
*And give the conception to the Trinity.*

St. Brigid's feast day was set on the Irish Celtic festival of Imbolc, which may have been a festival of the goddess. Imbolc marked the end of winter, the beginning of the season when, as historian Ronald Hutton says, "night is banished from the afternoon," the first buds

BRIGID CROSSES

appear, and ewes begin to lactate. The name of the festival contains an ancient Irish word for "milk" or "milking" (remember that St. Brigid is the wet nurse of Jesus).

A criss-crossing complex of symbols and meanings weaves Brigid's feast and Candlemas together. Inside the Irish word for "milk" is an even older root word that scholars believe may have signified purification. The day after Imbolc is the feast called the Purification of St. Mary the Virgin when, according to Hebrew custom, she went to the Temple in Jerusalem forty days after Christmas for ritual purification following childbirth. The Roman month name, *Februa*, means "purification," and it was the time for Roman rites of cleansing.

On St. Brigid's Eve, we can recognize customs we've seen at other times of the year. Irish families leave cakes for Brigid on their windowsills, or ribbons fastened outside the window for Brigid to bless as she passes. Girls weave crosses out of rushes or straw and hang them over doors or windows, or from the rafters, as a sign of welcome. (The patterns are rarely the conventional Christian cross, but are similar to certain prehistoric rock carvings.)

The most beautiful description of the evening's ceremony is given in Alexander Carmichael's *Carmina Gaedelica*. The woman of the house stands on the front step with her hands on the doorpost, and calls out, "Bride's bed is ready." Another woman behind her responds, "Let Bride come in, Bride is welcome." The woman in the door then says, "Bride, Bride, come in, thy bed is made. Preserve the house for the Trinity." "Bride, Bride, come to my house tonight. Open the door for Bride and let Bride come in," responds the woman inside.

The girls of the family fashion a sheaf of oat or corn husks into human form and dress it with rags or doll's clothes, seashells, and stones—the *dealbh Bride*, "icon of Bride"—and lay her in the *leaba Bride*, the "bed of Bride." They set a willow wand beside her. Before the family goes to bed, they smooth out the ashes in the hearth. In the morning, they look for the imprint of the willow wand or, better yet, Bride's footprint in the ashes. (Clement Moore did not invent the practice of supernatural entities coming and going by way of the hearth.) Out in the barn, old women might set bread, cheese, a jug of ale, and a lighted candle for Bride.

On Brigid's Day, the girls of the village, dressed in white and with their hair unbound, take the dealbh Bride from house to house and are given bannocks (a sconelike bread), butter, and cheese. Then they go back to one of their homes, bar the door, and feast. Later, the young men ask admittance and pay their respects to the dealbh. The dancing and merry-making go on until dawn.

In England, the cult of St. Brigid was strong at Glastonbury Abbey, one of the oldest and greatest cathedral-monastery complexes of Britain. That "holiest erthe" of English legend is associated dimly with a prehistoric female deity, the site of the Celtic otherworld, the Holy Grail, and King Arthur.


In Judaism, as in a number of other ancient traditions, childbirth made a woman ritually impure. The mother was required to go to the Temple forty days after the birth and to make an offering of doves. (In legend, St. Brigid accompanies Mary to the Temple.) The Torah also required that every firstborn son be dedicated at this time to Yahweh in memory of how he had spared the Hebrews' firstborn in Egypt. This is the event that the Western Church commemorated on February 2, in the Feast of the Purification of St. Mary the Virgin, or the Presentation of Christ in the Temple.

The spiritual center of the story comes when the old man Simeon, praying in the Temple, recognizes the infant Jesus as the Messiah. Simeon prophesies that the child will be a "light to enlighten the nations"—a universal savior.

The Church developed a ritual from its reflection on this idea, and from the character of the season. This was the procession of candles, from which the other name of the feast, Candlemas, comes. It was practiced throughout the Christian world from at least the seventh century until the Protestant Reformation. Every parishioner was given a candle; just before dawn, there was a long candlelight procession around and then into the church ending at the altar, where each candle was blessed with holy water and incense. At home, candles were lighted and set on windowsills to bring luck to the household throughout the year. The ritual symbolized Christ as the Light of the World, and the emergence of light in the natural world.

There's a grab bag of suggestions as to why the Church set this festival on this date. The most simple and obvious answer is that the Torah said the new mother should be purified

*Night Procession in Brittany,* by Ferdinand Du Puigaudeau (1864-1930).
*The candles of Candlemas are the gathering light of early spring.*

on the fortieth day, and February 2 is forty days after December 25. But is it coincidence that it falls on (or next to) the festival of Imbolc? As we've seen, the name of the Celtic holiday has an archaic meaning related to purification. The Saxon church chronicler Bede maintained that the pagan Saxons, as well as the Irish, had an important February festival.

Earlier (and to this day in Greek Orthodoxy) the feast of Candlemas had been on February 14. Pagan Rome did have a festival in the middle of February, the Lupercalia, which celebrated female fertility and featured torch-lit processions. As we've said, the Latin word *Februa* meant "purification," and the month was a time for cleansing rituals. But Lupercalia had been gone for centuries by the time Pope Sergius I decreed the candlelight procession at the end of the seventh century. There's no clear connection as there is, for instance, between Christmas and the Roman Birth of the Unconquered Sun. As with other feasts, they just seem to fit, evocatively, tantalizingly, with the sense of the season.

Liturgically, Candlemas marks the end of the first great cycle of the Year of the Lord and the beginning of the spring season, pointing toward the first events of the Easter cycle. In the days when the full Christmas cycle was observed, Candlemas was the day for taking down and burning Christmas greenery. With the presentation of the child in the Temple and the emergence of his mother from childbirth sequestration, the birth process is completed. In the psychology of the season, the bridge across the darkness has been successfully negotiated.

As with other Church holidays, especially those that absorbed some older indigenous festivity, Candlemas developed its own folk customs. Inevitably, this took the form of another variation of the ubiquitous nighttime visitors. In a rite similar to those for Brigid in Scotland, north Wales had Candlemas carolers. Groups of young men came singing to the doors of the cottages; to gain entry they would have to answer a set of riddles posed by the householder, and on this night they minded their manners. When they were admitted, there was a young woman seated in a chair with a child in a candlelit room. The young men came in and bowed to the "Virgin," before making their way back into the night.

This is obviously a lot like what would have been happening the night before on St. Brigid's Eve up in the Western Isles of Scotland, when the boys would have to beg admittance in order to reverence the Brigid icon. Once again the embroidery of linked themes and images presents a pattern, but the separate threads resist being pulled out. Is the Welsh Candlemas custom the influence of Brigid from across the Irish Sea? Whatever the process, the result is a festival honoring woman, spread across a wide area, as warmth comes back into the year.

Candlemas and the feast of Brigid are set at one of the four cross-quarter days of the year, which marked the opening of the seasons in prehistoric Britain and Ireland. In Ireland they were called Imbolc, on February 1 (spring); Beltane, May 1 (summer); Lughnasadh, August 1 (fall); and Samhain, November 1 (winter). The vestiges of the cross-quarter days in the Church calendar range from a major feast (All Saints) to a mostly forgotten bit of church lore (Lammas on August 1), to no trace at all (Beltane/May Day probably never had any hope of getting past the church door). The cross-quarter days are tuned to earth and weather, not to the solstices and equinoxes. They don't correspond to events in the life of Christ, which are set to the journey of the sun. They are based on lunar cycles and the feel of the seasons. They are folksy, rooted and local, concerned with herds and crops, events in the cycle of agricul-tural—not astronomical—life.

The reformed Church in Britain was predictably hard on Candlemas. The candlelit pro-cession and the blessing of the candles were the first to go, since the purpose of the ritual, in the eyes of the reformers, was the creation of superstitious talismans or charms. The spiritual and imaginative function of the rite was dismissed. Finally, the entire feast was banned by Elizabeth in 1559. Like All Souls, in certain regions it simply went outdoors or into private homes. In the Scottish borderlands, farmers set the gorse and heather on fire to substitute for the splendor of candles in church. More quietly, other households gathered around lighted candles in the longer evenings of early spring. But by the end of the eighteenth century, the special traditions of Candlemas had all but disappeared.

## Entering the Season

**Walking the Labyrinth**—The devotional/contemplative practice of walking the labyrinth was initially promoted by Canon Lauren Artress of Grace Episcopal Cathedral in San Fran-cisco and is becoming a widely popular spiritual practice. Walking a labyrinth pattern set into a cathedral floor seems to have been a medieval monastic aid to contemplation. It is a potent pattern that evokes prehistoric symbols, Marian devotion, and the pattern of sacred time, a prayer form that comes out of the feminine side of the sacred imagination. You can locate the labyrinth nearest you at the website for the Labyrinth Project of Grace Cathedral, at <www.gracecathedral.org/labyrinth/locator/index.shtml>.

**Brigid Crosses**—These are made in prehistoric patterns from wheat, corn husks or rushes, traditionally woven by children on the saint's day. They are feminine counterparts of the Celtic cross. There are instruction for how to make them at <http://www.bcpl.net/~hutmanpr/briget.html >. *Brigid of the Gael*, by Conrad Bladey (Hutman Productions, 2000) has a wealth of information about Brigid, including instructions for crosses and other ideas for keeping her feast. It may be ordered online at <http://www.ncf.carleton.ca/~er719/thesaint.html#main>.

**Transitions**—An idea from John and Caitlin Matthews, scholars of Celtic lore: find a stick or pole several feet long. Pound it into the ground in a part of your yard that gets the morning sun. Mark on the ground or in the snow the top of its shadow at the same time each day. Do this every few days, between Candelmas and St. John's Day, to become more aware of the sun climbing in the sky and to see how winter becomes summer.

**Caring for animals**—St. Brigid is a protectress of animals. There may be a free or emergency veterinary clinic near you, or a service that takes in injured wild animals. There is certainly a Humane Society shelter. All these need volunteers. Offer your help to them, of time or money.

**Reconciling opposing ideas**—Build an intellectual bridge between two apparently antithetical notions while respecting their distinctness. See if you can build a seamless bridge between the prolife and prochoice visions, for instance. This is the work of peace. See if this will work in a conflict to which you are a party.

## READING

Alexander Carmichael, *Carmina Gaedelica* (Lindisfarne Books, 1992). Alexander Carmichael worked for the Scottish national revenue office in the late nineteenth century, a job that required travel to remote parts of the Highlands and Western Isles. His real passion was to collect the stories, prayers, hymns, spells, and blessings that had been passed down for centuries in the Scottish Gaelic language. In doing so, Carmichael salvaged part of a remarkable culture that was then on the verge of disappearance. His book is usually a revelation to first-time readers, the discovery of an alternate world full of a strange—but also strangely familiar—music. There is a truly archaic and often magical atmosphere in these verses, but one that has fully interiorized the Christian symbolic world.

SPRING

# PART THREE

# SPRING

Spring, of course, is not a season of the Church Year—none of the four seasons of the natural year is. But it's interesting that no other season in the Year of the Lord hums with so much divine activity as springtime. Spring contains a large part of Lent; Holy Week; the Triduum of Maundy Thursday, Good Friday and Holy Saturday; the entire season of Easter; and the climax of the Christian year, Pentecost, marking the descent of sacred fire from Heaven.

If Christianity was truly an ascetic, antinature sort of creed at heart, as its opponents sometimes claim, you'd think the Church would have avoided this coincidence. Instead, the great events of divine life happen against a background of flowers and fertility, of the giddiness and liberation of spring. The awakening and fresh lightness of spring is a clue to the meaning of the liturgy, its life and energy.

Even in the darkest part of Lent, during the days that Christ lies in the tomb, we follow the lead of grass and flowers, gathering our forces down in the dark, learning about the growth that comes in the blind waiting till we are ready to rise up laughing in a slow explosion of light and greenness.

The central symbol of Christianity is the hideous torture stake, but spring shows us (as the old Fathers wrote long ago) that the cross is really a cutting from the tree of Paradise; in the spring rain it comes alive with flowers and green leaves. Jesus, the dead holy man, is carried into the final dark of the tomb, but overnight the tomb becomes a womb, and an impossibly promising new world emerges in the morning—the season of softness, pleasure, delight, and high spirits, of release from captivity, of unleashed energy, and the scent of lilacs. The poetry of Christmas contrasts the hidden light and the vast dark. In spring, there is no contrast between ritual and season—they merge into harmony. The divine drama sweeps nature up into itself.

*The Annunciation,* by Henry Ossawa Tanner, 1898. *A peasant girl says yes to the vast mystery, and everything changes.*

# 8

# MARCH 25

## THE ANNUNCIATION OF THE LORD
## (LADY DAY)

*I say that we are wound*

*With mercy round and round*

*As if with air: the same*

*Is Mary, more by name.*

*She, wild web, wondrous robe,*

*Mantles the guilty globe . . .*

*And makes, O marvelous,*

*New Nazareths in us,*

*Where she shall yet conceive*

*Him morning, noon, and eve . . .*

> —Gerard Manley Hopkins,
>     "The Blessed Virgin Compared
>     to the Air We Breathe"

*Church bells beyond the stars heard,*

*the land of spices, something understood.*

> —George Herbert, "Prayer"

*St. Gabriel to Mary flies,*
*this is the end of snow and ice.*

    —traditional rhyme

*O Mary, Mother, we pray to you;*
*Your life today with fruit was blessed:*
*Give us the happy promise, too,*
*That our harvest will be of the best.*
*If you protect and bless the field,*
*A hundredfold* each grain must yield.

    —Austrian prayer for the day of the Annunciation

## The Experience

She speaks for the humble and oppressed of the world. She is for the overthrow of the strong by the weak. She consoles and heals the world's wounded. It's important to understand this about her at the beginning. In an ecstasy of song she tells us:

*The arrogant of heart and mind he has put to rout,*
*he has torn imperial powers from their thrones,*
*but the humble have been lifted high.*
*The hungry he has satisfied with good things.*
*The rich he has sent empty away.*

Later, her son would claim that it was easier for a camel to go through the eye of a needle than for a rich man to enter the Kingdom of Heaven. At whose knee do you suppose he learned that?

It's been said that for most of its history, the Church has been pulling drowning people out of a river; but that now its job is to search upstream for those who've been throwing them in. Mary would agree. Revolutionaries wear her image in Ireland, Latin America, and Poland. She has always been the patroness of the poor. Remember, this unwed peasant mother from an impoverished village and her little family, like millions of people today, fell afoul of power. Shortly after the birth of her first child, they narrowly escaped a politically inspired massacre carried out by a local militia. For a time they were stateless refugees in a foreign nation. Eventually, her first-born son came to the attention of the occupying power, was arrested, and tortured to death in public.

It is hard to oppress people who value themselves, and for centuries, Mary has blessed the poor with a sense of their own worth. Nevertheless, even today nice people tend to think of Marian devotion as a little déclassé. The statue of Mary in the back yard—or worse, the front—makes us wary.

Spring equinox is the point at which darkness and all the hopelessness it represents are overthrown. Mary reminds the oppressed that the scales are about to tip in our favor, that the light has come back against the overwhelming winter darkness. "Those who threatened the child's life are dead," as the angel tells Joseph in Egypt.

To a philosophical citizen of the Empire in the first century C.E., it might have seemed that civilization was ordained to become more and more masculine. Jerusalem, Athens, and Rome were hard places, in thought and in action. The masculine logic of worldly power says that there are expendable souls—it must be that way for the world to work. The illogic of Christian love, born out of Mary's beleaguered family, says that there are no expendable souls.

In the spiritual imagination, the idea that all souls are precious had to be expressed in the figure of a divine woman and mother. To do this, the Church reached deep into the dream and myth life of the peoples around it. It was only a matter of time before a woman clothed with the sun would appear in the Christian heavens.

There can't be much doubt that Mary took on traits and titles of older female divinities as her spiritual function became more important to the Church. For instance, Isis, the great goddess of Egypt, depicted with her son Horus sitting in her lap, prefigures the iconic Madonna and Child of Byzantine art. Embodied in Mary, however, is a new development of spiritual imagination springing from the divine women of the past. Archaic goddesses symbolized fertility and nurture, yet they also stood for death and destruction. They were womb and tomb, the dark maw of the earth. Mary does not bury and devour. Through eyes of infinite compassion, she releases. She lets go of her firstborn to follow his path, no matter how her heart will be broken.

Mary stands at the gate of spring in both lunar and solar calendars—where prehistoric Europeans reckoned the opening of spring, on the cross-quarter day at the beginning of February (the Purification), and she is here at the vernal equinox.

Mary is the Gospels' most important image for understanding creativity and fertility.

*Mary and Isis*, by Luc-Olivier Merson, 1889. *The image of Mary and her son resonated with similar images in other, older cultures in ways that helped people understand the new Christian message.*

Mary says *yes* to the angel, to God, and at that moment she conceives Christ. A new world begins to take form. The Bible's vision of how creativity happens is when fire (also called "wind," "breath," or "spirit") and water come together. This is the drama enacted in the rite of baptism, when a candle is immersed in the baptismal font. The horizontal surface of the water meets the vertical fire coming down. They make a plus sign, a positive. Yes. The cross. The book of Genesis describes the beginning of creation by saying, "The Holy Spirit (or breath of God) hovered over the face of the deep." Jesus repeats this formula when he says that you enter the Kingdom of Heaven by being born of water and spirit. This simple equation unlocks Heaven in our minds. It is the process that initializes every creative act.

In ancient Jewish religious thought, great events repeatedly occur at the vernal equinox.

It is the anniversary of the first day of creation, when the spirit hovered over the water. It was also the time of Israel's liberation from Egypt, when the east wind blew over the Red Sea and parted the waters, one of the world's central images of freedom. Just as Mary sings about the powers being overthrown, the Hebrew slave girls dance on the shore of the Red Sea and bang their tambourines, singing, "The horse and rider he has thrown into the sea!"

And it is the time of the conception of Christ, when the Holy Spirit overshadows the woman Mary. Mary is the sea (*mare*, as the sea is called in Latin). The spirit broods over the waters.

In a number of Near Eastern mythologies, creation comes out of mortal conflict between male and female. The high god battles with the sea—personified as a sea monster—and destroys her, rending her body and scattering the pieces, which become the created world. The humanizing tendency of the Judeo-Christian tradition transforms this imagery. The spirit (or breath) of God *hovers* over the water and life springs forth. Mary isn't browbeaten into submission; her *yes* is essential to the process. It is central to the meaning of the story that she could have said *no*. There is a sense, as C. S. Lewis saw, in which we are all female in relation to the Divine.

There is a beautiful tradition among ancient Christian writers of symbolically playing with the image of Mary as the moon, the ruler of waters on earth. In ancient cosmologies, the orbit of the moon was the borderline between our temporal world and the eternal realm of the sun and stars. The moon became a symbol of Mary, who connects us to Heaven. She has one face toward the human world and one toward eternity.

As we saw at All Hallows, Mary is the great symbol of the middle realm, the creative, imaginative sphere through which God enters our hearts and our awareness. She is whatever *embodies* God—a piece of music, a lover, a prayer, a pet, a movie, a friend, a poem, a morning in summer. Mary is the source of creativity, just as the moon is a source of poetic inspiration. Gerard Manley Hopkins compared Mary to air, and this is a revealing way to think of her. In space, where there is no atmosphere, everything is either night or blinding light. On earth, the light of the sun is diffused through the atmosphere, so we can look up at the sky or see the whole world. This is why Mary's cloak is sky blue. At the vernal equinox, she mediates the growing light.

In the Jewish calendar, Passover comes at the first full moon after the vernal equinox. All those great events layered together at this time—the creation, the liberation from Egypt, the conception, the Resurrection—can happen only when the moon turns fully toward the sun, pregnant and fruitful with light. The Paschal full moon, glowing in the spring sky, symbolizes what is beginning on earth. The earth says *yes* to the increasing sunlight, the fire from heaven, and becomes green with new life.

Mary presided over the spectacular awakening of Western culture in the thirteenth century, the age of troubadour poets, St. Francis, Bernard of Clairvaux, Gothic cathedrals, romantic love, chivalry, and the Holy Grail. A strange new lightness came into the warlord world of northern Europe from that southern crescent along the sea. Like a warm breeze, it wafted up through Spain and Italy and found a special home in the south of France. The hearts of Islamic mystics burned for a celestial woman personifying God's wisdom and grace. Thus, from the gardens of the Alhambra in Moorish Spain comes the image of a lady seated in the heart of a lush garden—a suggestion of the sensuous spirit of the Song of Solomon. "The land of spices, something understood," as an old poet-priest would write centuries later, deep in the English countryside.

In the poetry of the Provençal troubadours and those that came after in the "sweet new style," there is a mixture of images and feelings that reflects both the new importance of Mary and a new feeling between the sexes. (It's similar to the way that gospel singers of the black church transferred the language of divine love to human love songs when they moved into pop music in the 1950s and 1960s. This gospel fervor accounts for the sweetness and moving power of great soul singers like Sam Cooke, Otis Redding, and Aretha Franklin.)

Things between the sexes have never been the same. Courtly values introduced the idea that there is a potential for transcendence in romantic relationships. It was a strange, almost occult notion—that men and women see the Divine in each other when they are "in love," that Eros is a special channel for grace—and it was an idea that forever changed our sense of the parameters of happiness.

The age of chivalry seems quaint and distant now; we take its values for granted because, in our time, its work has long been done. It's easy to miss how wonderfully odd and upside-down the notion really was, strange as a butterfly leading a tank column, the ladies dominating all those heavy metal warriors. Something was changing—these were still brutal times and brutal men, but there was a sense that even the most formidable fighter was answerable to a woman's gaze.

Suddenly the sullen fighting men of Europe began forming mystical-warrior orders dedicated to a woman. The knights in their sheets of armor on their huge steeds learned to dance, they learned gaiety and poetry and artful courtesy. In the literature of the time, they were troubled by immortal longings and disappeared on quests, looking for the fabulous Eastern cup that held the blood of God.

The brutish stone blocks of Romanesque and Norman churches underwent an alchemical transformation. Suddenly the stone took on light and life, leaping upward in the still-incredible Gothic Cathedrals dedicated to the Lady, weightless under her soft blue mantle of sky. Love poets appeared everywhere; Lancelot and Guinevere slipped off together; Robin Hood and Maid Marian flitted through the greenwood. Dour England began to be Merrie. Further south, young Francisco Bernardone of Assisi heard the music and threw off his clothes in front of a judge, to the mortification of his family. He found a Lady and became her troubadour, a juggler of God, and began to dance his way to sainthood.

The image of the rose haunts both the cult of Mary and medieval love poetry. The rose is a living mandala, a reflection of the wholeness of God in its perfect blossoming, its roundness, its revolution around a center that keeps opening up to depth after depth. *The Romance of the Rose* is one of the great works of chivalric love poetry. It is set in a dreamlike world where a lover wanders into a secret garden in search of a rose.

This hidden garden shows up again and again in the West, in dreams, fairy tales, poetry, scripture, mysticism. In Latin it's called the *hortus conclusus*, the walled garden. It isn't walled to keep people out, but to keep the mystery safe. True lovers can find their way inside, though the way might not be easy or clear, just as the prince finds his way through the forest of thorns to Sleeping Beauty's castle. In medieval art, this hidden garden symbolized Heaven and featured a clear pool with a fountain in the center. Mary's garden is where the spring of living water rises.

One of the great exploits of the nineteenth century, comparable, it's been said, to space exploration in our time, was the search for the source of the Nile, the great fertilizing river that made the oldest civilization possible. The reason it captured the popular imagination is probably because it acted out a myth. The pith-helmeted British explorers were looking for the hidden fountain. A poet once called the Mediterranean Sea "the blue pool in the old garden." At the origin of things we always look for the fountain, the deep over which the spirit broods.

Men look for it in women and all humans look for it in God. To find the rose is the desire that drives all souls. In the heart of the rose are refreshment and new life. The focal point of the Gothic cathedral is the spectacular psychedelic rose window at the western end of the transept—the goal of our procession and vision. The mystic rose of the Lady is both the heart and desire of chivalry.

In Christian myth, the redemption of the universe hinges on one young woman saying *yes*. March 25th is the holiday of *yes*, when the earth makes that jump over the halfway point. The cycles of earth and sun and planets are more than symbols. The universe behaves in certain ways because God behaves in certain ways; the physics of the spirit works not just in our hearts, but in the physical universe, too. Love steers the stars, Dante says. Maybe at the vernal equinox, the earth acts from love and not law.

The compassion of Mary is a face of God, but it has ramifications. It makes demands. It says, "Insomuch as you have done it to the least of these, you have done it to me." It says woe to us if we cause one of the little ones to stumble. Mary is the opposite of the pride of the world. She stands for the small things that overthrow the mighty, the buds and shoots that show so little strength and promise at first, but that will crack the concrete and transform the world if we allow the power of the spirit to move through us, if we just say *yes*.

## *The Story*

The Jews, as we've seen, believed that the vernal equinox was the time of great turning points, anniversaries, and analogies, each succeeding event mythically reenacting and developing the previous one in new and unexpected ways. First, it was the time of the creation of the world, when God established the balance of night and day. Next, it was the time of Israel's liberation from Egypt, when the spirit of God again hovered over the waters to create a new nation. Ever since, the Jews have celebrated their central feast of Passover in harmony with these images. They also believed that the vernal equinox would, at some time in the future, see the passing of the old world and the beginning of the reign of God.

Passover came to be reflected twice in the Christian calendar. As we've seen before, the Church for centuries could not decide when to celebrate the Resurrection. Should they assign the feast to the vernal equinox in the Roman solar calendar, or affirm the ancient link with the wandering moon of the nomads and use the Jewish lunar system?

Eventually the Church went with the connection to Judea and the moon. But they held onto the second date and to Jewish traditions surrounding the vernal equinox. The Church added to this series by setting the Resurrection (the beginning of the new creation) at Passover, which they later called Easter. But to the equinox itself, they assigned the conception of the Savior.

Devotion to the Virgin Mary grew gradually from the early decades of the Church, along with the status of this woman so crucial to the redeeming work. Old instincts of religious imagination were brought to this imaginative process after having been discouraged for centuries in official Judaism. One of the great ideas of Second-Temple Judaism was to spiritualize Yahweh, to refine him from an anthropomorphic Middle Eastern monarch with consort and court into a transcendent universal spirit. As a side effect, however, all female divinity disappeared along with Yahweh's heavenly court. This spiritual vacuum was filled, once the Church moved into the heterogeneous religious world of the Empire, by a lush and fast-growing flowering around the person of Jesus' mother.

The transformation of the Galilean peasant girl into an object of veneration is one of the more remarkable processes in the history of religion. In the Gospels, Mary, after her encounter with the angel at Jesus' conception, is never assigned supernatural attributes or actions. She does not play an active role in Jesus' ministry. Yet sometime in the years following her death, people began praying to this woman. In a genuine popular religious development, she became the Mother of God, Queen of Heaven (as Astarte, goddess of the Phoenicians, had been known), the lady who hears the cries of the world with a mother's heart.

Theologically and mythologically, the role of Mary grew dramatically. By the time of the Council of Ephesus in 431 c.e., she had been given the Greek title of *Theotokos*, or "God-Bearer," raising her to the status of a cosmic figure. In working out the implications of this role, the Church formed the basis of Marian devotion and theology.

The High Middle Ages (around 1100 to 1300 c.e.) saw the first real flowering of Western culture after the collapse of Rome. The cult of Mary, which reached its zenith in this era, influenced the development of the new civilization.

Courtesy and chivalry, signaled by the deliberate holding back of the use of force and a gratuitous turning toward beauty and refinement, were the signs of increasing social complexity and sophistication. For a warrior to join and enjoy the society of women, he had to cultivate radical new behaviors. This was the real beginning of northern European civilization, and it grew under the influence of Mary.

To postfeminist Westerners, the cult of courtly love and chivalry seems laughably idealistic, even reactionary. We have heard a lot in recent years about the "madonna-whore" polarity in the attitudes of our culture toward women. It would be a mistake, however, to impute those motives to the world of chivalric Europe. If worship of woman today implies as its shadow contempt and fear of women, remember that for much of history the contempt and fear were already there—it was the worship that was new. The exaltation of the feminine that began with the medieval cult of Mary began a process that over time would do a lot to heal and balance relations between the sexes. It's why Western women don't walk a step behind their men.

Why and how this new energy emerged at that time has been debated for centuries. It first flourished in the warm south of Europe, and it has been suggested that it may have come from lands warmer still, from the world of Islam. The art and thought of Moorish Spain had a tremendous influence in Europe. The Sufis, Islam's mystical sect (well-represented in Spain), venerated a divine principle called, in Greek, *Sophia*, the wisdom of God, whom they imagined as a supernaturally beautiful woman. The warmth of their devotion may have enlivened the feeling for Mary and for women in general.

What's certain, as historian Otto Vonn Simson says, is that "the age was indeed the age of the Virgin." The enormous revolutions in art and sensibility were linked with her. The great Gothic cathedrals are not only dedicated to Mary, they are, in a sense, representations of her. Mystically and mythologically, Mary is identified with the Church.

The Protestant Reformation, with its radical distrust of Mary (and any other holy image besides that of Christ) was a return to the Second-Temple distrust of images in general. The Oxford Movement in Britain among English Catholics, led by John Cardinal Newman, was a nineteenth-century reaction to this aridity, an attempt to restore sacred imagination to the Church.

In 1950, the Roman Catholic Church made a momentous decision. In an era when Protestant and Catholic theologians were working hard to reconcile the conflicts of the Reformation, the Roman Church elevated the bodily Assumption of the Virgin Mary to the level of official doctrine. This was a striking extension of the semidivine status of Mary. In some important ways, it put Mary—theologically, imaginatively, and in devotional practice—on a footing close to that of Christ.

In orthodox Roman doctrine, there is only one entity in Heaven that has a corporeal body, and that being is Jesus Christ. (All the human souls in Heaven are disembodied; they await the final trumpet for their bodies to be resurrected.) To say that Mary was translated bodily into Heaven at her death is to make her the only other being in the cosmos who has this savior-like nature of being eternal and embodied at the same time. This comes strikingly near—shockingly near, in Protestant eyes—to saying that Mary too is a divine being—what Protestants had feared all along was the real tendency of Marian devotion.

What might have seemed in the eyes of the secular world to be a rather obscure and reactionary tinkering with doctrine was, in the eyes of depth psychologist Carl Jung, a major development in the spiritual history of Western man. It was a revolutionary restoration of the feminine principle to the sacred imagination. Jung saw it, not as a defiant assertion of old-fashioned Romanism, but a wise incorporation of the yearnings and wisdom of the people, who had been living with this sentiment for centuries.

Mary today remains one of the most popular aspects of Catholicism, indeed, of Christianity. She lives deeply in the imaginations, spiritual needs, and desires of millions. There are people in every country and in every century, including the twenty-first, who have talked to or seen the Virgin. Their experiences tend to be similar. She typically appears as a shining young woman (often not immediately recognizable as Mary) in a remote place near a natural grotto or spring. She often appears to children and usually bears an urgent spiritual message, either for the witnesses or the world at large. Some of the sites of these apparitions have become world-famous pilgrimage destinations and places of healing—Guadalupe in Mexico, Fatima in Spain, Lourdes in France, Medjugorje in Bosnia-Hercegovina; Knock in Ireland.

Mary attracts much contemporary interest, from theologians to New Agers, as a feminine face of the Divine. One of the best-known examples of modern Marian devotion comes from the most famous rock band of the counter-culture sixties. This was of course, the Beatles hit "Let It Be," written and sung by Paul McCartney. The Beatles had a knack for absorbing and reflecting whatever milieu they were in. Perhaps because of the heavy Irish immigration into Liverpool, Paul instinctively expressed his sentiments in Catholic language. "Let It Be" is, apparently, an account of a Marian apparition.

> *When I find myself in times of trouble,*
> *Mother Mary comes to me,*
> *speaking words of wisdom,*
> *"Let it be."*
> *And in my hour of darkness*
> *she is standing right in front of me . . .*

As in the classic Marian apparition, she delivers a message:

> *And when all the broken-hearted people*
> *living in the world agree,*
> *there will be an answer,*
> *"Let it be . . ."*

Though McCartney's simple voice-and-piano arrangement was layered over by producer Phil Spector's garish choir and kitschy ecclesiastical trappings, "Let It Be" remains quite moving, especially when one knows that McCartney's mother, who died when he was a boy, was named Mary. It spoke powerfully to a generation of young people who had unnerved and exhausted themselves, yet were still troubled by spiritual longings.

## Entering the Season

**Retreats**—There are monasteries, abbeys, and retreat centers (many run by orders dedicated to Mary) throughout the United States that welcome individuals making a retreat or pilgrimage. See *Sanctuaries: A Guide to Lodgings in Monasteries, Abbeys, and Retreats: the Complete United States*, Jack and Marcia Kelly, (Bell Tower, 1996); or *A Guide to Monastic Guest Houses: Fourth Edition*, Robert Regalbuto (Morehouse, 2000). If you don't find anything nearby in these guides, call your local Roman Catholic or Episcopal diocesan office.

**Gothic cathedrals and rose windows**—These mighty structures express the loving mysteries of Mary and the Holy Spirit in stone. The upward-reaching vault of the nave pulls one's sense of self into a new configuration—larger, lighter, more *oriented*. At the end of the great cavern of light the vast rose window breaks the sun into a paradise of color. This is the architecture of prayer and spiritual fertility, as the light of the Holy Spirit enters the womb of the church through the heavenly rose.

**The labyrinth (again)**—The labyrinth, part of the spiritual treasure house of the Gothic, is the celestial rose on the ground. If you could fold up Chartres Cathedral like a doll's house with hinged walls, the rose window would directly cover the labyrinth, the same dimensions to within a couple of feet. Pilgrims on the labyrinth way also wander within the heavenly rose.

**Praying the rosary**—The rosary, the practice of saying a set pattern of prayer to the Virgin while counting the beads of the rosary chain, is one of Marian devotion's important contributions to contemplative practice.

## MUSIC

Sinfonye with Stevie Wishart, *The Courts of Love: Music from the Time of Eleanor of Aquitaine* (Hyperion UK CD 66367, 1990).

Altramar, *Saint Francis and the Minstrels Of God* (Dorian Discovery CD80143, 1996).

Anonymous 4, *An English Lady Mass* (Harmonia Mundi France CD907080, 1993).

The Robert Shaw Festival Singers, *Evocation of the Spirit* (Telarc CD80406, 1995).

## READING

C. S. Lewis, *The Allegory of Love: A Study in Medieval Tradition* (Oxford University Press, 1985). No one equals Lewis at bringing alive the mind and mood of medieval writers. Here he writes about the expansion of Western consciousness that was expressed and developed in the literature of courtly love.

G. K. Chesterton's *St. Francis of Assisi* (Image Books, 1987) is a concise, very readable introduction to St. Francis, whose life traced the high points of medieval spirituality. It's also not a bad introduction to this great Catholic wit and *bon viveur* of early twentieth-century England.

In *The Mary Myth: On the Femininity of God* (Seabury Press, 1977), Andrew Greeley, Chicago's acerbic, novel-writing priest, unfolds the many meanings of Mary. (Out of print; available from libraries.)

*EASTER MORNING*, BY CASPAR DAVID FRIEDRICH (1774-1840).

*A NEW WORLD HAS BEEN BORN IN THE NIGHT; THE WOMEN GO TO SEE.*

# 9

# THE SATURDAY BEFORE EASTER

## EASTER VIGIL

*I begin by the grass*

*to be bound again to the Lord*

  —A. E. (George William Russell), 1867–1935

*This feast of the Spirit leads the mystic dance*

*through the year.*

  —Hippolytus, Easter Vigil hymn, third century

*0 night of more delight than is paradise . . .*

*night of all nights in all the year desired,*

*night of the church's bridal . . .*

*Night when the heir took the heiress*

*to enjoy their inheritance.*

  —Asterius of Amasia, fourth century

*May the light of Christ, rising in glory,*

*dispel the darkness of our hearts and minds.*

  —Lighting of the candle, Roman rite

# The Experience

Like most children, I learned what sacred time was like from Christmas. We may know that Easter is the oldest and the primary festival of the Church. Compared to Christmas, however, the imaginative impact of Easter, for most of us, is minor. Clergy grant this somewhat reproachfully, as if we've been lured from due respect for Easter by the glitzy charms of Christmas.

But it's not glitz that's made Christmas the dominant festival. How could Christmas not be popular? People will cling desperately and flock wildly to anything that gives them a taste of sacred time. The real question is, why doesn't Easter offer us this experience?

I think the problem is that hardly anyone goes to the Easter Vigil.

English historian Ronald Hutton maintains that the spread of Christianity into northern Europe made the greater popularity of Christmas inevitable. It seems obvious that the mood of Christmas has its primary source in the winter solstice—in the terrific imaginative impact of the death and rebirth of the sun as seen from snowy forest and moorland. After all, we know that people were celebrating the winter solstice long before they were observing Christmas. But the mystique of Christmas has another source as well.

Historically, Christmas was a transplant of Easter into midwinter, duplicating the form of Resurrection observances to celebrate the birth—the "Winter Pascha" as the Eastern Orthodox Church calls it. In particular, the sacred time of Christmas Eve was a midwinter mirror of the sacred time of Easter Eve—of the Easter Vigil. Our experience of Christmas has its root in the ancient Easter mysteries as much as in the drama of a northern midwinter. Christmas took on the popularity of Easter because it took on its mood and atmosphere. This is a key to making Easter come alive imaginatively.

Although it may seem backwards from a historical and theological point of view, one way to climb back inside Easter is to start at Christmas. We come out the other end at the Easter Vigil.

The real holy, magical hours of Christmas are on Christmas Eve—a theological and liturgical truth that all children know. It's the same with Easter. The birth and the Resurrection both happen at midnight, on the eve of each festival "when half-spent was the night." Christmas morning and Easter Sunday are after-the-fact celebrations of the enormous thing that happened in the night. To celebrate a full Easter without the Vigil is like trying to celebrate a full Christmas without Christmas Eve.

But let's start by thinking about the imaginative *differences* between the two holidays. I'd put it this way: Christmas feels timeless; Easter feels ancient.

We don't know the actual date of Jesus' birth. The feast falls where it does to coincide with astronomical events that have been going on since the earth was formed; like the Incarnation that it celebrates, Christmas comes from outside human time and history.

Easter is different. The Gospels are precise in the dating of the Crucifixion, and they name the particular Roman colonial administrator who ordered it. At Easter we relive events that are fixed in historical time. We're in first century Palestine—with the dust and heat, the stones of the streets and the marble floors, the temples and forums, the jangle of armor and brass of trumpets; feeling the elation, suspense, sweat, fear, pain, horror, grief, wonder. Easter is a strange tale from far away and long ago that comes to us with trappings of its exotic and ancient setting. At Easter we're back in that crucible of consciousness, the Middle East and the old Mediterranean world.

But Christmas Eve and the Easter Vigil are twins—two movements of one drama. The two stories are both set inside a cave, symbolized by the cavernous church. The dark church of Christmas Eve is the cave of the Nativity, of winter. This dark world is the womb of time where the miracle gestates.

At the Easter Vigil, we pick up where we left off on Christmas Eve—we re-enter that dark space. Now it's Jesus' tomb, the "nightmare of history" that James Joyce talked about. The world that Christ entered at Christmas has hardened around him, trying to seal him off from us. He has entered it so deeply that it seems impossible to get out.

In these two caves at the two midnights, at the darkest hours, eternity arcs into time. The sacred flame that the priest kindles at the Vigil says that it is happening *here*. The bells that the congregation ring at the moment of Resurrection say that it is happening *now*. In the cave of the Nativity, Christ is born *into* time from eternity. In the cave of the tomb, Christ is delivered *out of* time and into . . . everyone. Both nights are the birth of Christ. At Christmas, the one Christ is born. At Easter, all the little Christs—the newly initiated—are born.

The seasons teach theological lessons. We walk out of the Christmas cave into the depths of winter. At Easter, we walk out of the tomb into the garden to encounter Mary Magdalene, symbol of the redeemed springtime world. She has been waiting out there for all the Christs born at Easter midnight. "Come away, my love," she says in words from the Song of Songs. "It is spring and the voice of the turtledove is heard in the land."

*It is the spring of souls today,*
*Christ has burst his prison,*
*and from three days sleep in death,*
*as the Sun hath risen.*

—John of Damascus, eighth century

Just as spring is beginning, just as the world opens up and calls us to jump in, we turn away; we set aside the three days of the Triduum to prepare to enter the "life" part of the year. We go underground like seeds and roots, like the dead. We gather ourselves for the great thing about to happen. There is the sense of huge events proceeding around us:

*Something strange is happening—there is great silence*
*on earth today, a great silence and stillness. The whole earth*
*keeps silence because the king is asleep.*

—*Office of Readings,* Roman Rite

At the Easter Vigil, we participate in the processes of the universe. As we go up to take communion and the choir sings "Now the Green Blade Riseth," we're following a pattern that even the grass obeys. We have the chance to enter the story from which all stories come.

Easter hallows its season, and the season hallows Easter. Season and festival, natural cycle and spiritual cycle, complement each other to create sacred time. On Easter Eve as on Christmas Eve, we sit again in holy darkness. Our Christmas candles, the little Christmas stars, are now gathered together into the "new fire" of Easter. They are given to everyone, never to be extinguished.

## *The Story*

It is early spring in 33 C.E., in the Roman province of Judea, just a few years since the execution of Jesus of Nazareth. A small group of people is meeting in secret on this spring night. A few days earlier they celebrated Passover, sharing the seder meal with their families. Now they're gathered in a cave in a rocky hillside in the open country between Jerusalem and Bethany. The Sabbath ended at sundown. It is near midnight, already the first day of the week, the day the Romans dedicate to the Sun, which people here have started to call "the Lord's Day."

*The Morning of the Resurrection, by Sir Edward Burne-Jones (1833-98).
At the Easter Vigil, we reenact the ancient drama;
the miracle happens here and now.*

They are one of a number of cults that have a peculiar slant on Jewish prophecy and worship. People are starting to call them Messianists, because they believe their late rabbi to have been the *Messiah* or Anointed One promised in prophecy to redeem the Jewish nation. No one here has any thought that there will ever be a written account of Yeshu Massias, Jesus the Anointed. Most of them, in fact, will be dead before the first gospel writer sits down to transcribe the story.

Since they don't share their master's penchant for the dramatic public gesture (and resulting public disturbance), the Roman administration has largely forgotten about them. But ever since their master's execution, the Jerusalem religious authorities have watched them with a wary eye. They appear to be meek and ultradevout—some of them are almost always in the Temple. But the priests are aware that their beliefs are developing in bizarre, even blasphemous, directions. Some outspoken members of the cult have already been stoned to death for impiety or heresy. A systematic effort to eradicate them will soon begin. Meanwhile, there's a distinct possibility they could all be executed if they're caught. The ritual about to take place would confirm the priests' worst suspicions. They are about to celebrate one of the first Easter Vigils. It is a reenactment of their Lord's Resurrection.

They have been sitting here in the dark through the first hours of the night in the black cave, so reminiscent of the cold stone tomb in which the ruined body of their master was laid. During that time, the rabbi has recited from the Books of Moses the story of how the Children of Israel passed through the waters of death and came out a new people on the other side, the waters slamming shut on the dark old power of Egypt forever. They have chanted some of the beautiful psalms of King David.

But the early spring night is cold. Water drips; it smells dank. Sitting against the rough walls is uncomfortable and legs are cramped. Things rustle and scuttle in the dark. They think more and more of the tomb, of being laid in the cold dark forever. They think about the mob with stones in their hands, the way people get bolder and move in closer, clutching their rocks, after the first stones have stunned the victim.

Then, at the darkest hour, halfway through the night, there is a sound: the scrape of a flint. Suddenly light blazes. The leader, one of Jesus' companions, has lit straw and kindling in a brazier. "The light of Massias," he chants. It is the very moment when divine life entered the stony tomb outside the walls of Jerusalem, imperceptible to the sleeping soldiers and the sleeping priests. It is the darkest hour of the night—the moment dawn begins—at the season when the world begins to awake from winter.

One by one, the people bring candles and oil lamps forward and light them from the flame. Soon the cave is transformed from a tomb to a wonderland. The air is rich with incense. The walls glow in the golden light. The faces above the flames are radiant. Now new candidates for the cult are brought forward for the rite that will initiate them into the resurrected life that Yeshu Massias is now living. This will enable them to survive the approaching destruction of the world. The candidates have been praying, fasting, and studying. Tonight they will stand naked before their brothers and sisters, naked as they came into the world, naked as their master when he died. They will descend into a pool where the waters of death will close over them, as King David sang in the Psalms, and they will come out "born of water and the spirit." Like newborns, they will be fussed over—embraced, rubbed with scented oil, given names, fed with milk and honey, wrapped in soft white robes.

After that it gets worse, if that is possible, from the point of view of the Temple. The group will share a meal in which the bread and wine, they somehow believe, is the body and blood of the resurrected Jesus. This too, like the baptism, joins the initiates to Him and to his timeless life.

The Easter Vigil is the central and (aside from the sacrament of baptism) the oldest Christian ritual. In the first Christian centuries, it was called "The Night of Illumination," "The Night of Radiant Splendor," or "The Great Service of Light." It was the *only* time of the year at which candidates were baptized, as if the precise anniversary of the Resurrection opened a channel between aspiring Christians and the Kingdom of Heaven. All initiated Christians, in fact, experience the renewal of the Christ life again at this time. Jesus' first followers celebrated it when the Crucifixion and Resurrection of Jesus were still shared memories, well before the written Gospels. They used the form of the Passover Vigil to celebrate Christ's passing over from earthly to eternal life.

As years went by, whole communities gathered for the Vigil, and the celebration lasted the entire night. Baptism took place around midnight, and the Vigil ended at sunrise with the first Eucharist for the newly initiated. As Christianity became established in the Roman world, entire cities were illuminated for the Vigil. In homes, in churches, even in the streets, candles and lamps were lit by the thousands—one of the great spectacles of an age when night was really dark. A contemporary writer describes how, in Milan, the emperor Constantine "transformed the night of the sacred vigil into the brilliance of day by lighting throughout the whole city pillars of wax, while burning lamps illuminated every house, so that this nocturnal celebration was rendered brighter than the brightest day."

In later centuries, in old Christian Europe, there was an electric air of expectation on Holy Saturday. As at Christmas Eve, children would watch for the first star. After the long, grueling fast of Lent, they eagerly awaited the first signal that fast was over and feast begun.

After the Reformation, the Roman Catholic Church moved the celebration of the Easter Vigil to Holy Saturday morning, which vitiated its imaginative and spiritual impact. In the 1950's, Pope Pius XII restored it to the night. In many parts of Europe, even today, homes are darkened in anticipation of the Vigil, each family carefully putting out every light in the house. After the Vigil, a piece of holy fire, in the form of a candle lit from the fire at church, is brought back home to relight all the household fires, filling and sanctifying the house with light.

The idea of a sacred flame that provides light for all people, especially at springtime, goes very deep in human hearts. The British historian of seasonal customs, Ronald Hutton, says in *Stations of the Sun* that "the custom of a ritual of renewal whereby all fires in a community were put out and relit from a single, freshly kindled, sacred flame was familiar alike to the Incas, Mexican natives, Inuit, African and Indian tribes, Russian peasants, and the civilizations of China, Japan, ancient Greece, and pagan Rome." Fourth-century pilgrims to the Holy Land were the first to record the rite of the Easter fire in the liturgy of the churches in Jerusalem.

There is another story that the Easter flame came from Ireland. The tribes of Britain and Ireland celebrated the beginning of spring with huge bonfires, but early Christian missionaries suppressed the custom. St. Patrick, however, incorporated the druid Beltane fire of spring into the Easter rite. When Irish monks went to the continent in the sixth and seventh centuries, they brought along this tradition, setting and blessing bonfires outside the church on Holy Saturday night. According to this version, the custom became so popular that the Church eventually incorporated it into the liturgy, and the lighting and blessing of the fire became the first act of the Easter Vigil.

However the fire entered the liturgy, the tradition of an outdoor bonfire on Easter Eve lasted long in Europe. In France, boys would build the fire in front of the church, each adding a piece of fuel to which they had fastened a strand of wire. After the priest had lit and blessed the fire and the logs were burning, each boy pulled out his own log and ran home to light hearthfire, stove, candles, and lamps. The charred sticks were thought to bring protection from storms and lightning throughout the year.

## *Entering the Season*

**Participation in Holy Week**—Take part in all the services of Holy Week. They are one great drama and have a cumulative effect.

**Keep Holy Saturday**—The Roman Catholic Rite of Christian Initiation for Adults says, "The elect should be instructed that on Holy Saturday they should rest from their ordinary work as far as possible, spend time in prayer and recollection of mind, and fast according to their ability." Think of Holy Saturday as a Christmas Eve when you don't have to wrap packages.

• Watch for the first star.
• Have the children search out and turn off every light in the house before you go to church.
• At church, put your candle in a tall holder to protect it from wind and bring it home to be

the first new light in your home, to light candles or a fire; send the children around the house to turn the lights back on.

- Have a special dinner when you get back from church.

## MUSIC

George Frederic Handel, *The Messiah*. London Symphony Orchestra, Sir Colin Davis conducting (Philips 420 865-2,1966).

Johannn Sebastian Bach, *The St. Matthew Passion*. Philharmonia Orchestra and choir, Otto Klemperer conducting (EMI CDMC 63058,1961).

*Great Music of Holy Week and Easter*, the *Choirs of St. Mark's Cathedral, Seattle, Washington*, J. Melvin Butler, organist/choirmaster.

*Easter: Gregorian Chant by the Monastic Choir of St. Peter Abbey, Solesmes*, from the European center of Gregorian tradition. It may be ordered at <www.solesmes.com>.

Peter Gabriel, *Passion: Music for The Last Temptation of Christ*. This highly evocative soundtrack musically puts the Passion story back into its native culture.

John Fahey, *Yes, Jesus Loves Me* A collection of well-loved American hymns from the late, eccentric master of folk guitar.

There's no mistaking the sweet and bracing beauty of Shaker songs like "Simple Gifts"; "How Can I Keep from Singing?" or "Come, Shaker Life." *The Golden Harvest*, Joel Cohen and the Boston Camerata (Glissando CD20, 2000) is an excellent sampler.

"John Barleycorn Must Die" from Traffic, *John Barleycorn Must Die* (1970). Nineteenth century folklorists called it "The Passion of the Corn."

There is no substitute for classic African-American gospel music. Try the late Reverend James Cleveland, the Soul Stirrers, Edwin Hawkins, or the Fairfield Four; Sweet Honey in the Rock does sublime *a cappella* updates of the spirituals tradition.

The Beatles' "Here Comes the Sun" is the good news according to John, Paul, George, and Ringo, from their farewell album.

*THE PENTECOST, BY LOUIS GALLOCHE (1670-1761). AT PENTECOST, THE LIGHT OF CHRIST IS DISTRIBUTED TO EVERYONE.*

# 10

# SEVENTH SUNDAY AFTER EASTER

## PENTECOST (WHITSUNDAY)

*The wind blows where it wills;*

*you hear the sound of it,*

*but you do not know where it comes from,*

*or where it is going.*

*So with everyone*

*who is born from the spirit.*

— Jesus, John 3:8

*It is summer, summer, the heart says,*

*and not even the full of it.*

— William Carlos Williams,

"The Ivy Crown"

*Are we supposed to take all this greed and fear and hatred seriously?*

*It's too consistent. It's like watching dust settle.*

— T-Bone Burnette

*And tho the last light off the brown brink westward went,*

*the Holy Spirit o'er the bent world broods, with warm breast,*

*and with Ah! bright wings!*

— Gerard Manley Hopkins

# The Experience

Over the head of every man and every woman dances a flame.

The noise of the great rushing wind, the tongues of fire, the voices speaking in language of such power that everyone in the streets of every nation can understand. These images are as big and compelling as any of the central dramatic acts of the Gospels, as strong as Christmas and Easter.

But Pentecost is different. In the great vignettes of the life of Christ in the Gospels, the main actors are people, and there is a poignant human light in the stories. But Pentecost is more similar to huge natural forces: a cosmic breaker crashes over some confused folks who've now been left behind twice—once at the Crucifixion and again, just days earlier, at the Ascension. Yet at the same time, these big forces become individual and personal. Each man and woman is given their own flame.

The Nicene Creed, which many Christians recite every week in church, basically lays out the roles of the three members of the Holy Trinity. It introduces God the Father; it clarifies the relation of the Father to the Son; it summarizes the life, death, Resurrection and Second Coming of Jesus Christ. And then it disposes of the Holy Spirit in two sentences: "With the Father and the Son he is worshipped and glorified. He has spoken through the prophets."

Whoa. The rhythm and syntax are rather like a person getting to the part of a family story that contains something difficult but unavoidable—"And then there's my younger brother Phil. He does something for some people in Costa Rica. . . ."

Now I'm not saying that this was the intent of the august churchmen who gathered at Nicaea. But I think it's telling that nothing at all is said about the action of the Holy Spirit in the lives of believers—about what it *does*; about, as the theologians say, its place in the work of salvation.

"The wind blows where it will," Jesus says to the Pharisee Nicodemus, one of the religious authorities of Israel. So it is with those born of the Spirit. He's telling Nicodemus that there's finally no knowing with people whose actions are like the wind, whose inspiration isn't determined by the false choices the world offers. People who don't wear Blake's "mind-forg'd manacles." It is an image of indeterminability and of great freedom.

The Holy Spirit is power to the people. Each person has his own source, her own connection. You can understand how the folks at the Council of Nicaea, whose purpose was, after all, to define uniformity in the Christian religion, may have been a little uneasy with tacking on a coda to the effect of, "Oh—and also, all baptized Christians have complete and utter freedom in the fullest and most radical sense."

The Holy Spirit is at the center of the Christian way. It is the living element, the operative mechanism for relating to God. It is that part of ourselves that is related to the Divine. The whole point of Jesus' life was to send the Holy Spirit. "If I do not go away, the Paraclete cannot come to you." The person who develops a relationship with the Holy Spirit, who lives a life open to it, is at the place that Christian story, theology, and practice want us all to be.

The Holy Spirit is that part of the action of God that exists within each person's subjective awareness. It is inspirer, guide, director, comforter, source of strength. It's the source of all religious experience, from mystical rapture to a simple sense of guidance or presence. It is the means by which people know and feel God. It leads us, like Jesus said, into all truth. When people express their own understanding of religion or communicate their faith or spiritual experience, they may refer to feeling "something inside" them. That's the Holy Spirit.

At Pentecost, freedom is declared. The month of May is the first taste of the summer ahead, and Pentecost the feast of first fruits. Summer is the symbol and sacrament of Paradise, the world as it is meant to be. Pentecost/summer is the rightness of the world restored.

The project of Christianity, as the early Christians saw it and as you can read in Paul's letters, was the restoration of Paradise. The first Christians (who thought that before they died, the hosts of Heaven with Jesus at their head would appear in the clouds and roll up the sky like a scroll) were a little off in believing this literally, but they were right to take seriously the idea that Christianity is about reclaiming the full, natural relation to the Divine that existed in Eden. The Book of Revelation describes this Paradise as a day with a sun that never sets—a summer day. The dark parts of the cycle are in the past.

Every mood and turn of meaning of the liturgical year reflects some truth. In the world of time, the way to symbolize an eternal truth is to have it recur. Just as we are always going through the dark from Michaelmas to Christmas, just as we are always dying between Good Friday and Easter, we are always being restored to our divine nature, as dramatized by Pentecost.

There is an implication in the theology of Pentecost that the Church doesn't address. That is the fact that, theologically, the work of Christ, of salvation, is accomplished at Pentecost. The large and subversive message is that we are restored to Paradise. Take some time with this. Pentecost tells us that the world-restoring work of Christ is successfully accomplished. It just remains for us to realize it.

Of course there's always work to be done in the temporal world. Work, we learn in Genesis, is Adam's punishment when he gets kicked out of Paradise. But Pentecost is a symbol from the imagination of God that in the timeless world of the spirit, the work is eternally complete.

The hardest lesson of the spiritual life is that no work is necessary. We cannot get ourselves into Heaven. We must accept the fact that we are already there, and act accordingly. The Church's doctrine of the free gift of grace describes what all creative people—from plumbers to parents to poets—understand about their moments of inspiration. They are given to us. They are not the result of struggle. It is precisely when we give *up* that we are given *to*. An advertising creative director once said to me that, while it takes a lot of work to come up with a good idea, a great idea is no work at all. This is part of the Good News that the disciples could not proclaim until they had experienced Pentecost.

I am not the first one to point this out, but Christianity is not an especially sad, or even penitential faith, despite the demeanor of many of its adherents. "Joy," as Chesterton said, "is the great secret of Christianity." Asceticism, discipline, and penitence are useful tools, but worth less than nothing as ends in themselves. In the Bible, the Greek word that is translated as "repentance" is *metanoia*, which has the sense of turning in a different direction. Christian spiritual discipline is no more than remembering to turn at right angles to the time line and face into eternity, like a faucet turning to let the flow of water through. It's easier than jogging every morning.

The upshot of this is that we don't have to save the world—it's been saved already. When the Church talks about how "Christ has won the victory," it's serious. This should be part of every Christian's awareness. We just have to live in recognition of that fact. Despite our having to guard against evil and struggle for justice along the time line, there's nothing inherently wrong with the world from the perspective of eternity. One writer once said that tragedy is like an indulgence we're temporarily granted as we prepare to face the huge reality of joy. An adjustment needs to be made—an adjustment dramatized by the story of Christ —and we're there. The door opens into summer.

When Christianity came to northern Europe, Pentecost fused with the month of May, in which the feast most often falls. Once again, the year provided the poetry, a sacramental body for the spiritual event. The downpouring of holy fire from Christ at the center and height of the universe found its corollary in the slow turning of the season, as the sun finds the center and height of the sky, and new shoots and buds and blossoms turn their faces toward the fire from heaven. The poetry of Pentecost is the poetry of spring.

Pentecost is, in the language of the church, the start of the Green Season.

Pentecost is "Green Holyday" in Poland; "Flowerfeast" in Germany; "Summerfeast" in Slovakia—time for the most widespread and most assuredly prehistoric customs of Europe—decking homes, churches, and public buildings with flowers and greenery.

May 1 is one of the cross-quarter days, the archaic markers of the seasons. It was long considered, in intuitive response to the changes in the earth, to be the beginning of summer. The reveling with which people had always greeted the start of summer took its place in the round of the Christian year. Whitsunday, "White Sunday," is what the British called Pentecost. The May festivities became known as Whitsun Games, or Whitsun Ales (since the new beer had just been brewed).

Village people built a bower—a shelter of green branches and flowers—as the focus of their revels, and chose a "Summer Lord" from among the young men to be the master of the season's revels. There was also a Summer or May Queen, called the Pentecost Bride in Eastern Europe, as his consort.

The same strange cast of characters as at midwinter—the old man/woman, the fool, the hobby horse—emerged to dance and perform. And there was someone else, someone who, like the priest during Pentecost, also wore green.

Robin Hood, lord of the greenwood, the great outlaw hero of England, was famous by the middle of the thirteenth century. His story began with commoners and smallholding rural gentry. Nineteenth-century folklorists tried to identify him with one of a number of outlaws of whom there are existing historical records, or with members of the lower nobility fallen afoul of the monarchy. Others asserted he was an ancient woodland spirit. (There was, in fact, a famous woodland-dwelling, green-wearing fairy being known as Robin Goodfellow.)

Certainly Robin was the Summer Lord par excellence. Robin's ballads begin "in sumer, when the shawes be sheene" (in summer, when the leaves are green). In many communities, a local youth chosen to be Robin, along with his band, led the Whitsun revels. Robin was a strange but perfectly appropriate symbol of the new kingdom initiated on the earth at Pentecost. Shakespeare says of a similar band of outlaws that they live "as in the Golden Age,"

MAY DAY, BY EDGAR BARCLAY (1842-1913). PENTECOST, "GREEN HOLYDAY,"
"FLOWERFEAST," "SUMMERFEAST"— THIS IS THE DAY WHEN THE WORLD COMES ALIVE.

which is to say, the unfallen world. Robin's greenwood has whispers of Paradise; it is the Green World of literature and story, a close cousin of Paradise in the symbolism of the West. It is never winter in the greenwood. There is no want or hunger; there is no work (Adam's curse), just play. People live in trees. This is the Pentecost world, the world of the Green Season. Christ invited Robin of Sherwood into the dance, and Robin and Christ knew what his coat of Lincoln green was for.

The British Christian mystics, as Thomas Merton says, were "Paradise men" (and women). The British feeling for nature, whether expressed in religious language or not, grows out of a sense that Paradise is close under the surface of the natural world. A famous quote of Julian of Norwich, the fourteenth-century mystic—"All shall be well, and all shall be well, and all manner of thing shall be well"—comes out of the same sensibility.

Nature is the sacrament of the season. At Pentecost, we look at nature through redeemed eyes, our Christ eyes. Paradise restored is nature seen through unfallen eyes. The season of summer at the heart of Pentecost is the time when this is most obvious, and we partake in the sacrament of the season by taking advantage of it. The villagers built their Whitsun bowers as a reminder of the time before time, when all of nature was a temple. As it was in the beginning, it is now and ever shall be, world without end.

The story of Pentecost is one of the foundations for the idea of individual freedom. If Western culture has chosen freedom as the political state that best reflects human dignity, it is partly because one of the founding myths of the West is the story of Pentecost. But we need recurring Pentecosts to ensure that more and more of the spirit enters human life, to refresh and respiritualize our vision of freedom. The gospel songs of the black church that powered the Civil Rights movement were Pentecost songs. The 1960s may have been, generically, a pentecost.

> *After this I shall pour out my spirit on all mankind;*
> *your sons and daughters will prophesy,*
> *your old men will dream dreams,*
> *and your young men see visions . . .*
>
> —Joel 2:28

"It must begin here and now, a new continent of earth and fire," the Jefferson Airplane sang.

The early twentieth-century German mystic and founder of the Waldorf School movement, Rudolf Steiner, called Pentecost "the festival of free individuality." To him, Pentecost was connected with the development of human consciousness from group identification with family, clan, tribe, race, to the awareness of individual selfhood and a one-to-one relationship with the Divine.

Pentecost points the way to the future of Christianity, and symbolizes the next step in the ministry of the Church to the world. Pentecost is the happy ending. Music plays. The door in the sky is opened. The white light of Whitsun, the green leaves of summer, the living experience of God within us, the beginning of happily ever after.

## *The Story*

Some works of basic Christian instruction describe Pentecost as "the birthday of the Church." This is an insipid way to even begin to describe Pentecost. And it's another way to avoid dealing with the Holy Spirit, which in general is what Churchianity prefers to do. But let's back up.

Historically, Pentecost was, after Easter, the second major holiday of the Christian calendar. *Pentecost* is the Greek word for "fiftieth," the Greek name for the Jewish festival of Shavuoth, which celebrated the first fruits of summer. It was also called the Feast of Weeks because seven weeks (forty-nine days) go by from Passover to Shavuoth. The feast comes on the fiftieth day. The seed that buds at Pesach/Passover bears its first fruit at Shavuoth/Pentecost.

The early Jewish followers of Jesus naturally continued to observe the festival. They came to associate the first Shavuoth after Jesus' death with an enormous event in the development of their tradition. In reflection on what they had been through, it seemed to the early Christians that the point of Jesus' life, death, and resurrection was that, once he had become part of eternity, Jesus could mediate a new power or possibility to them. Pentecost became the symbol of this new potential granted by Christ. The first mention of Pentecost as an official Christian holiday is from the third century in the Eastern Church.

In a sense, Easter and Pentecost are two ways of exploring the same spiritual developments. Easter is an image of the new spiritual life as expressed in the individual life of Jesus of Nazareth. Pentecost depicts the experience of the new life communally. Another way of looking at the story of Easter/Pentecost (as suggested by Gretchen Wolf Pritchard) is that Easter is not the finale of the Jesus drama—Pentecost is. On Easter, Jesus is still in transit. He has not arrived at his destination; he has not "gone to the Father." In his Resurrection appearances to his friends, he's stopping off. At his Ascension, the work is complete, the circuit closed: God has gone down into the world to be embodied in human nature; now human nature ascends into eternity. With this work completed, the transformation of humans can take place—at Pentecost. Jesus' followers are, in the image from Luke, "enlightened"—the illumination has come upon them. Allan Watts points out the echoes between the Pentecost imagery in the Acts of the Apostles and the yoga image of the sun door in the top of the head.

Pentecost in the Jewish tradition is said to be, among other things, the anniversary of the day that Noah's Ark came to rest and the flood that had destroyed the world subsided. Part of God's promise to Noah is that he would never again destroy the world with a flood. The next time, God says, it will be with fire. The Pentecost story takes that image and does a trick with it. God pours fire down on the world all right, but not like in the days of Noah. John the Baptist, angry prophet of the end who predicts the baptism of fire that will burn the chaff with unquenchable flame, may have been misunderstood. A baptism of fire there is, and it will ignite the world, but it will transform and not destroy.

In summer, the world around us is full of life. The boundary between us and nature is fuzzier than in winter, when we stand out in sharp relief against a frozen landscape. If we were viewed through infrared goggles walking down our icy streets, we would look like little red fireballs against a dark background. In summer, the boundaries are softened; we melt into the surroundings—the level of life all around us has risen close to our own. Jesus said that he came so that we may have life and have it abundantly. Nature does this in summer.

It bothers literal-minded Christians that we might take the invitation of Pentecost seriously and stop working out our salvation with fear and trembling, stop bearing the old rugged cross, stop hoeing our hard rows. But this is what it's all about. We are supposed to lay our burdens down, enjoy the glorious liberty of the children of God, let the truth set us free (you can muster just as many quotes on one side of this as the other, you see). Pentecost and summer are the sacraments of the eternal Sabbath of rest—which we are seriously supposed to be enjoying right now. School's out, summer vacation. Endless summer. The "unimaginable zero summer."

One of the most elaborate pieces of church dramaturgy was saved for Pentecost. Medieval churches often had a "Holy Ghost hole" in the ceiling, a trap door just for Pentecost effects. Through it would come white doves (the traditional symbol of the spirit), rose petals, flowers, and sprinkled holy water. Then a great disk the size of a cart wheel—painted the blue of the summer sky with golden sun rays and in the middle, the dove of the Spirit—would be lowered on chains and swung in widening circles.

Of course, the ritual aspect went away with the Reformation. The Whitsun revels and ales declined from the seventeenth century onward. But the Protestant churches did not reject everything. The core of Protestantism affirms the spark of divinity given to each of us, our living connection to the Divine, taking precedence over all churchly hierarchies. Even out at the far reaches of Protestantism among the Pentecostals, in the strange shouts in the night from the Holiness Church on the corner, we can still feel a far-off breath of Pentecost, the wild inspiration blowing where it will.

## *Entering the Season*

**The merry month of May**—The oldest folk rite of Pentecost is the gathering of greenery and flowers, which like the disciples, turn their heads to the light. The heart of the May ritual is to go out before dawn. Take your children to a forest. Gather some wildflowers and green branches and bring them home. This is called "Bringing in the May." Gather flowers from your garden and leave baskets of them on your neighbor's doorstep. The dew on the morning of Pentecost has a special blessing. Distilled, purest water, it catches the light and becomes drops of fire. Tell your children to gather the dew in small bowls, or soak it up in a clean white cloth. Wash your faces in it.

**Breath**—The word *spirit* is from the Latin *spiritus*, meaning "breath," which is a translation of the Hebrew *ruach*, the word used in the Bible to refer to the Spirit of God as well as ordinary human breath. There is a sense in which the Holy Spirit and human breath are related to each other and work together. One of the most basic (yet richest) methods of meditation uses the breath as a focus. Simply paying attention to the breath flowing in and out of your nostrils is all there is to it. Do this for as long as is easy for you. (Many teachers recommend twenty minutes.) There isn't a better exercise for developing holy attentiveness.

**Inspiration**—To be inspired in the Bible and in early Christianity was to be an open channel for the Holy Spirit—God breathing through you. We all have moments when we feel inspired. When the solution to some problem is given to us; when we are "on," those moments when we can do no wrong; the wind has caught us up. The essence of inspiration is that it cannot be made to happen. But can we court these moments? We can certainly invite the spirit, as the great chant of the Church says, *Veni Sancte Spiritus*—"come, Holy Spirit." In a way, that's the whole Christian spiritual life in a nutshell, to invite the Holy Spirit whenever we think of it. Pentecost is the perfect time to draw aside and think of simple ways to invite the action of inspiration.

**The sun**—The sun is one of the deepest and oldest symbols of God It became a symbol of Christ very early in the story of the Church. At Pentecost the sun becomes the central symbol of the Christian year; the feasts from now until Michaelmas look to the sun as the primary symbol of Christ and the divine life. We don't mourn him, we don't look anxiously for his birth. He is here in his fullness. Pay attention to the sun, as the early Church certainly did.

SUMMER

# SUMMER

*S*ummer is the season of recognition, the season of presence. In summer all potential is realized. Nature is naturing, *natura naturans*, as the Scholastic philosophers said; everything is everything, as the hippies said. The world has reached fruition, yelling a silent green yell in our faces to wake up. Nothing is hidden. The presence, which was sadly fading in the fall, achingly far in Advent, is right before our eyes.

In summer readings from the Lectionary, we relive the earthly time of Jesus outside the great world-saving acts of the Christmas-Pentecost half of the year. These were the days that began with Jesus making more wine for a wedding feast, days of joy and celebration, when the bridegroom was present with his friends.

The discipline of summer is to develop unfallen eyes, the ability to see the presence of the Kingdom, to see that the Divine is right here right now. This is the art of contemplation, and summer holds in its center the patroness of contemplation, Mary Magdalene.

The Green Season is not, like most of the liturgical cycle, dramatic. Drama comes out of conflict, the struggle of light and dark. Summer has not been accorded great sacramental meaning by the Church, but it is there anyway. Summer is the sacrament of Kingdom Come.

In summer, we are close, face to face with the bridegroom. Summer contains three feasts to honor people who had "eyes to see" the mystery in front of them: John the Baptist, who sees that the young man from Nazareth is "the lamb of God"; Mary Magdalene, who sees that the gardener near the nightmare execution ground is really the risen Christ; Peter, James, and John, who, on the top of Mt. Tabor, see in their friend the glory that always is. Summer contains the climax of Pentecost and of the year. At the end, we ascend a mountaintop where the light is full and the view is far.

Up there, a new path begins, the first steps of the next cycle.

*THE SERMON OF ST. JOHN THE BAPTIST, BY PAOLO VERONESE (1528-88). JOHN THE BAPTIST, PATRON OF THE SUN AT ITS HEIGHT, DECLARES THE KINGDOM HAS ARRIVED.*

# 11

# June 24

## THE NATIVITY OF ST. JOHN THE BAPTIST
## (ST. JOHN'S DAY)
## MIDSUMMER

*What, it will be asked, When the sun rises do you not see*
*a round disk of fire somewhat like a Guinea?*
*O no, no, I see an Innumerable Company of the Heavenly host crying*
*"Holy, Holy, Holy is the Lord God Almighty."*

—William Blake

*When he came upon a great quantity of flowers he would preach to them and*
*invite them to praise the Lord, just as if they had been gifted with reason. So*
*also cornfields and vineyards, stones, woods and all the beauties of the field,*
*fountains of waters, all the verdure of the gardens, earth and fire, air and wind*
*would he, with sincerest purity, exhort to the love and willing service of God. In*
*short, he called all creatures by the name of brother, and in a surpassing man-*
*ner, of which other men had no experience, he discerned the hidden things of*
*creation with the eye of the heart, as one who had already escaped into the*
*glorious liberty of the children of God.*

—Thomas of Celaso, on St. Francis

*The Kingdom of Heaven is spread out upon the earth,*
*but men do not know it.*

—Gospel of Thomas

## *The Experience*

Israel is a Mediterranean country, like southern Italy or Greece. True, it perches on the edge of the desert, and from Jerusalem it's not a long walk into the wilderness. But while some parts are arid, others get rain and turn lush and green in spring and summer, especially in the northern region called the Galilee. Remember, this is the land flowing with milk and honey.

The Gospels are told as a string of separate incidents, aphorisms, and stories tacked into a narrative. We don't get much sense of day-to-day life among Jesus and his followers. Hearing the Gospels when I was little, I filled in the blanks (as I think other children have) by imagining a kind of extended ramble across hills and streams and dusty villages, stopping by springs or wells in the heat of the day to cool off and talk. It must have been fun, I thought, as they marched across the summer hills. It sounded like a wonderfully light life.

And then at night, there always seemed to be a feast. By some sort of holy coincidence, Jesus' band always finds someone to invite them to dinner. Out of nowhere come meat, bread, and wine (maybe even music); friends and strangers gather around, and the talk begins.

The kickoff of Jesus' ministry in the Gospel of John is the famous wedding in Cana, where he miraculously provides more wine for the embarrassed host after the guests have drunk up the supply. The central image—really, *truly* the central image—of Christianity is the festive table, the wide-open impromptu dinner party, and this apparently goes right back to the lifestyle of Jesus and company. In the Gospels, people are frequently disconcerted by this—it's not quite what they expect a holy man to be doing. How can they fast when the bridegroom is with them? Jesus blithely responds.

The things that sound harsh in their lives (Jesus' command to carry no purse and no staff; no possessions, essentially) don't feel like austerities, but rather the requirement for traveling light. That the Son of Man has nowhere to lay his head is not, in these circumstances, such a bad thing. You can see it as an idyll of vagabonding, like the carefree honey that people distilled out of misery in songs from the Great Depression. "When you ain't got nothin', you got nothin' to lose," as Bob Dylan put it. It's a way of turning poverty to an advantage, and I think this may be part of what Jesus was talking about when he said that the poor have a special blessing.

This period of day-to-day life as part of Jesus' little society tends to fall below the liturgical radar. The high points, the big dramas of birth, baptism, transfiguration, death, and resurrection, are the events that punctuate the spiritual year. There's wisdom in this structure, but we miss something if we don't see that this dinner-party interlude, the feast time, is also important.

The summer readings in the liturgy are from the summer of Jesus' earthly ministry. This eternal summer of walking the Galilean hills and valleys was not really a "foretaste," as theologians say, of the glorious post-Second Coming new earth. This was the genuine article—a small-scale working model of the Kingdom in action.

It strikes a person, looking at the Church Year, that there's a great big void over on the other side of the circle from Christmas. With the Christmas festival, the Church wove the winter solstice deep into the Year of the Lord. But the summer solstice just isn't set into the Christian imagination.

There is something, though. In the Gospels, John the Baptist is born six months before Christ, and so the Church gave John—Jesus' cousin, mentor, forerunner—the position of honor at the opposite side of the year from Christmas, at the summer solstice.

"He must grow greater as I grow less," John the Baptist predicts of Jesus. This is one of those intriguing lines in the Gospels that seems to have more lurking behind it than is ever explained. John's words imply a sort of seesaw balancing act between Jesus and his cousin. Yet liturgically, the summer solstice is pretty lightweight. Do we step off the high point of Pentecost into nothing?

No, we step off into the kingdom of summer. Remember, John's work as described in the Gospels was to announce the Kingdom. As a prophet, John sees the world in the light of eternity, with unfallen eyes, because he is a creature of Paradise, one of the three people in Christian lore born without original sin—in other words, born to live naturally in the paradisal state. The season of summer stands for the vision of John. John, prophet of the Kingdom, rules over midsummer.

The poetry of happiness, it's been said, is the hardest poetry of all to write, and the Year of the Lord is an enormous poem. But in some ways the poetry of happiness can be the deepest of all. It's there in the summer if we have ears to hear and eyes to see.

Summer doesn't feel like a particularly sacred season. It's not an inward-looking time, but a practical, active, busy time. Just imagining a winter night puts a hush on our thoughts. The summer air by contrast seems full of sound, light, heat, birds, bugs. It seems at first to be the least poetic of seasons. It's all there on the surface. Summer is obvious. It's like a child's drawing, with a big yellow smiley face in the sky. But there is another summer.

At the high noon of the year, we feel something like the midnight expectancy of Christmas Eve, a tension of stillness. There's a hum, a presence that reminds you of the way you can tell that a TV is on in the next room even if you can't hear it.

A great kingdom is at its zenith. Even northern lands are connected, under the summer sun, with ancient sun-drenched lands of winged golden bulls and kings with golden masks. The dark golden-green paths in the summer woods hide secrets, like the halls of an emperor. The pointed green patterns of the summer leaves are an ancient alphabet, the hieroglyphs of Eden.

In the mythology of the Celtic people on the western fringes of Europe, one of the epithets for Paradise was "the summer country." The state of the world in summer is what the Bible calls "Beulah Land," the married land. There is a spell in the world come to fruition. Summer is the time when the hidden green life is most active, in the woods, under the level of the flowers. It is not a coincidence that summer impressed people in earlier times, in remote places, as the greatest time for fairy activity, since fairies are the imaginative distillation of life in the green world. Though we think of summer as the daytime of the year, there are no nights quite so charged as summer nights. A winter moon may be distant and beautiful, but a summer moon is a present force.

In earlier times, people responded with festivity. In the same way that old May festivities entered the Year of the Lord as Whitsun games, so prehistoric midsummer traditions became part of St. John's Day. Fire is the natural sacrament for most of the turning points of the year, but midsummer is fire's heyday.

The people of northern Europe used to wrap a spoked wheel in straw, set it on fire, and roll it down from the highest hill, hoping to land it in a stream (if one was available) at the bottom. Boys with sticks guided the wheel and kept it upright. At the end, the ashes and burned pieces were gathered and distributed to bring luck for the coming year. Historian Ronald Hutton has traced the written records of this custom back to the fourth century, and there is every reason to think that its origins are in prehistory. The flaming wheel continued to roll until the middle of the nineteenth century. The spoked wheel was the most common symbol of the sun in ancient northern Europe, and it entered Christianity as the Celtic cross of St. Patrick.

At St. John's moment of midsummer, the cross, where time and the timeless intersect, its arms going off in the four directions, takes on the completeness of the circle, the fiery wheel of the summer sun. The enormous dramas of Christmas and Easter have brought us here.

*Midsummer Eve*, by Edward Robert Hughes (1851-1914). *The midsummer triumph of the kingdom—seen and unseen, creation joins in the dance.*

We've played our parts. The work is done, the Kingdom is come. Summer invites us to the feast, like the one they enjoyed in Galilee in the presence of bridegroom.

## *The Story*

People who've grown up with Bible stories tend to take for granted things that strike new readers as needing a good deal of explanation. One of these is the figure of John the Baptist. The Baptizer is mentioned at or near the beginning of all four of the Gospels. He and Jesus are related—second cousins, in fact. Mary's cousin Elizabeth, in her old age (like Abraham's wife, Sarah) becomes miraculously pregnant six months before Mary's angelic visitation. John and Jesus are described in apocryphal accounts as having been playmates in the streets of Nazareth.

Later references indicate that John is well known throughout Judea. (The Jewish historian Josephus mentions his great popularity among the people.) Jesus thinks of no one more highly, and he receives John's messengers regularly.

So, to paraphrase the Sundance Kid, who is this guy? And why does he baptize the Son of God? The traditional explanation is that John's mission was to prepare the way for Jesus. His baptismal program is seen as a sort of preliminary, whipping folks into shape to get them ready to hear Jesus. But who was he in his own right, and why was this relationship with Jesus so important?

The scholarly consensus seems to be that Jesus was originally one of John's followers, and that Jesus' own ministry began as an offshoot of the Baptist's movement. Jesus' first followers were disciples of John, and Jesus carried on John's new rite of baptism. It is likely that Jesus saw John as his mentor and perhaps regarded him as such until John's death.

What was the message that attracted the young Jesus of Nazareth and laid the groundwork for his own mission? John spoke to the growing desire for individual transformation—the idea that a relationship with God had to come from something more than membership in the right tribe, nation, or race. (In this way his appeal was similar to the mystery religions of the Roman world, popular at the same time.) "Do not think to say, 'We have Abraham for a Father!'" John says. "God is capable of making children of Abraham from these stones!" Your group mythos was not enough; it wouldn't take you there. You had to—and you could—live it yourself.

John created a new rite to initiate individuals into this new awareness. This rite of symbolic rebirth—going under the water and coming out of it new again—acted out, on an individual basis, the great myth of Israel, of deliverance through the Red Sea and entry into the Promised Land.

The union of old midsummer and St. John's Day is another weaving of native tradition, with liturgy and theology that developed as the Church struck roots in northern Europe. The birth date of John the Baptist was, in part, set by the Gospels, which state that he was born six months before Jesus. Since Jesus' birth was celebrated at the winter solstice, it followed that John was born at midsummer. It did not follow, however, that the solstice would be his feast day. A saint's feast day is typically the anniversary of his death. Even Jesus' death and resurrection anniversary is a greater feast than his birthday. Not so with John. Unusually, the major feast of this major saint was set by the Church on his birthday.

Partly this is because, in orthodox belief, John, along with Mary and Jesus, was born without original sin. The significance of a saint's death anniversary is that it is the moment of his birth into Paradise. Since John is there from birth, his birthday is his spiritually significant date.

But the unusual dating of John's feast suggests that the Church may have also seen the symbolic potential of midsummer and of that half-year between John and Jesus. If the real birth dates of the two cousins were not known (and they most likely were not) then there must have been some meaning implied by the story of their births half a year apart. Certainly John's comment about Jesus, that "he must grow greater as I grow less," sounds like some kind of religious formula, a sense of rising and setting that evokes astronomic or seasonal cycles. The high earthly sun of St. John's Day becomes the hidden spiritual sun of Christmas.

In the Gospels, John represents the temporal human world at its best: "Among all those born of woman, there is none greater than John the Baptist," Jesus told his disciples. But anyone who participated in the new creation that Jesus inaugurated would be "greater," simply by being a part of it. John the Baptist had one foot in each world—he stood at the dividing line between history and the beginning of the Kingdom, the midpoint of the human story, just as his feast stands at the midpoint of the year and the beginning of summer.

The Feast of St. John was a time of festivity across Europe. Young people spent the night outdoors, an activity that Shakespeare immortalized in *A Midsummer Night's Dream*. The solstice sun rising at the same point in the sky for several days (in other words, time stopping) made it a good time for magic. As with the other major turning points of the year, the eve was especially charged. As at Halloween, the future could be seen—all time being, in theory, viewable from this point outside time. On the vigil of St. John's Day, hidden treasures were said to lie out on the open ground in lonely places, waiting for the seeker. Herbs picked on St. John's Eve had special healing powers, and it was a good day to cut divining rods to locate water under the earth. It was also an active time for fairies and other supernatural creatures.

Like the celebration of Christmas, the liturgy of St. John's Day included three masses: one in the middle of the night recalling John's mission as Precursor, the second at daybreak, and the third at midmorning. The whole sequence was almost as rich and elaborate as the rites of Christmas.

There was a custom of largesse from the wealthy to the poor. Squires set out tables of food and barrels of ale.

St. John's Eve was especially a time for fire. Dom Prosper Guéranger, abbot of the Benedictine monastery of Solesmes in France, writes this description of St. John's Eve in the nineteenth century: "Scarce had the last rays of the setting sun died away when, all the world over, immense columns of flame arose from every mountaintop, and in an instant, every town and village and hamlet was lighted up." On fishing boats from Brittany, sailors raised barrels of rags to the highest yardarm and set them ablaze at dusk, until the whole fleet was illuminated on the water. In the west of Ireland to this day, St. John's fires are a regular tradition.

In the cities there were fires in the streets. People hung lanterns outside their doors. Fantastic "watches," or parades, were held in the larger cities. A good example is the watch sponsored by the Drapers Guild in London in 1521. It featured giants, St. George and a dragon spitting fireballs; a "Castle of War"; Pluto, god of the underworld; sixteen naked boys "dyed black to be devils"; and a King of the Moors in black satin and a turban with white plumes; all of it accompanied by something referred to intriguingly as "wild fire."

In other parts of Europe, traditions (appropriately for the Baptist) focused on water. In Slavic lands, the name for the festival, *Kupalo*, comes from the word *kupati*, which means "to bathe." Masses of people would go to lakes or to the seashore at sunrise. The sun, as it "bathed" in the waters at the horizon, infused all water with its power. Anyone bathing on this day would absorb some of the blessing. The poetry of the Year of the Lord weaves the universe into a pattern; sun and sea become the candle and water that create the fiery water of the baptismal font.

*Jumping Through Fire*, by Alois Greil, 1889. On St. John's Eve,
*the kingdom of summer begins on earth.*

## *Entering the Season*

**Outdoor devotions**—We're not only given summer for recreation, but to enjoy sacramentally. Make a point to occasionally do your devotions—prayer, contemplative or meditative practice—outdoors. This is one way to develop unfallen eyes.

**St. John's Eve**—This is a magical night, though not a perilous one like Halloween. At St. John's, the victory of the light is assured. All creation, seen and unseen, can emerge and join in the dance of the Kingdom at the peak of the year. This includes fairies, for whom children should leave out bowls of milk. In return, they will leave some trinket. This helps a child imagine an unseen world that is good and part of God's creative pattern, as opposed to the many unseen worlds a child hears of that are merely scary.

**The Fourth of July**—We've talked about how calendar reforms adopted across Europe between the sixteenth and eighteenth centuries pushed dates backward by eleven days relative to the position of the sun. January 6 is called Old Christmas Day, and is eleven days later than contemporary Christmas. July 4 might be called old Midsummer's Day, eleven days from June 24. Are Independence Day fireworks a lost stepchild of St. John's Eve bonfires? No matter what the historical connection—or lack of one—the Glorious Fourth offers an opportunity to sample something of the mood of the old midsummer festivities.

**Fire**—While I wouldn't urge anyone to roll a burning wheel downhill (unless you own an awful lot of property) a bonfire is completely appropriate. St. John's Fires once burned all across Europe. Join with your forebears who set these sacraments of light to mirror the fire in Heaven.

**Water**—In the astrological scheme of time, the two-thousand-year cycle that began roughly around the birth of Jesus was the Age of Pisces, the fish. The symbol for Christ among early Roman Christians in Rome was a fish. Jesus, in gospel stories, is never far from water in some form. His followers were drawn largely from the fishing trade. And the great rite given to Jesus by John and passed along to his own followers is, of course, a water rite. To understand the play between the sensory and the symbolic, all you have to do is throw yourself into some water on a hot summer day. You really do feel like you've shed something old and worn out when you emerge from it. As Blake said, the natural world is that part of the Divine we perceive with our senses. A few moments in the water on a hot afternoon is enough to convince you that there is a living water.

**Paradise**—Do something creative about Paradise. Draw it. Make a miniature Paradise in a terrarium. Make a Paradise in your yard for your kids or yourself.

MARY MAGDALENE, BY ANTHONY FREDERICK AUGUSTUS SANDYS, CA. 1858-60. THE MAGDALENE—PASSIONATE SEEKER OF GOD, SWEET MYSTERY OF THE GOSPELS—WITH HER ALABASTER JAR.

# 12

# JULY 22

## THE FEAST OF ST. MARY MAGDALENE

*My beloved spoke, saying to me:*

*"Rise up my darling;*

*my fair one, come away.*

*For see, the winter is past! The rains are over and gone;*

*the flowers appear in the countryside;*

*the season of birdsong is come,*

*and the turtle-dove's cooing is heard in our land;*

*the green figs ripen on the fig trees*

*and the vine blossoms give forth their fragrance.*

*Rise up, my darling;*

*my fair one, come away."*

—The Song of Songs 2:10–13

*The springtime of Lovers has come,*

*that this dust bowl may become a garden;*

*the proclamation of heaven has come,*

*that the bird of the soul may rise in flight.*

—Rumi, thirteenth century

*O, the summertime is coming*
*and the leaves are sweetly turning,*
*And the wild mountain thyme*
*blooms across the purple heather,*
*will ye go, lassie, go?*

—Robert Tannahill, "The Wild Mountain Thyme"

*"Mariham, Mariham, the Happy . . . Speak in boldness, because thou art she*
*whose heart straineth toward the kingdom of the heavens more than all thy*
*brothers."*

—Jesus to Mary Magdalene, Pistis Sophia, third century

## The Experience

Mary Magdalene is a sweet mystery of the Gospels, one of those characters that seem to point to a whole other story that the evangelists decided not to tell. Like the man with the water jug who leads the disciples to the room of the Last Supper or the young man in the white linen loincloth who flees naked from Gethsemane when the soldiers arrest Jesus, these figures have no "back story," as the Hollywood screen writers say. They invite the imagination to fill in the blanks.

Mary Magdalene plays a more significant role in gospel stories than either of those figures. Though not an apostle, she's clearly important among Jesus' followers, closer to him by all appearances than some of the twelve. She is, after all, the first witness to the Resurrection, first to encounter the risen Christ, first to bring the message. She is known in Church tradition, in fact, as the Apostle to the Apostles.

Because of her mysterious aura, she has inspired a lot of imaginative activity, starting with early popes and Church fathers, who fleshed out a story and personality for her. More recently, some have seen in her (as in the Virgin Mary) aspects of female divinities, memories perhaps of one of the consorts of God in early Semitic mythologies. Mystically inclined feminist writers have seen her as the priestess of a goddess. Some have speculated that Mary, in her traditional role as a repentant prostitute, is connected to religious temple prostitution in the ancient Near East.

Regardless of these speculations, however, there is an ancient and strong tradition of a special relationship between Mary of Magdala and Jesus of Nazareth. Millennia before the furor over Nikos Kazantzakis' *Last Temptation of Christ*, she was envisioned metaphorically as the beloved or bride of Christ, a favored and intimate companion, a female "Beloved Disciple."

One of the most moving passages in the New Testament occurs in John, when Mary recognizes Jesus in the guise of the gardener, outside his tomb on Easter morning. How does she know him? By the way he says her name: "She turned round and saw Jesus standing there, but did not recognize him. Jesus said to her, 'Why are you weeping? Who is it you are looking for?' Thinking it was the gardener, she said, 'If it is you, sir, who has removed him, tell me where you have laid him, and I will take him away.' Jesus said, 'Mary.' She turned to him and said, 'Rabboni (my teacher)!'" (John 20:14–17) You have to be pretty hard-hearted not to feel an entire relationship in that sublimely simple exchange.

We know from the Gospels that Jesus rid Mary of seven demons (or impurities); that she was one of a group of female followers who accompanied the apostles in their wanderings; that she was present at Jesus' death; and that she met the risen Christ on Easter morning before any of the other disciples.

Church tradition depicts a Mary Magdalene who is a composite of several women in the Gospels: Mary Magdalene is practically a generic name for all the women in the Gospels who have significant interaction with Jesus. There is the sorrowing prostitute who crashes the Pharisees' feast to wash Jesus' feet with her tears, her hair, and a cruet of myrrh. There is the Samaritan woman at the well on a hot afternoon who offers the stranger a cool drink, who has had five husbands, and who has currently taken up with yet another man. There is the woman with the alabaster jar of costly ointment who uses all of it to anoint Jesus' hair and is rebuked by Judas for her extravagance. There is Mary of Bethany, who sits with Jesus while her sister makes dinner, getting a scolding from her sister and a commendation from Jesus. All these have been used to create the personality and story of Mary Magdalene.

It's perfectly appropriate for biblical scholars to distinguish between these characters, and many women would like to see Mary Magdalene cleared of what they see as the slander of having been misrepresented as a prostitute. But I wouldn't want to lose the composite traditional Mary Magdalene. She is a figure of richness and depth, a seeker of great boldness, openness, and passion, who acts unselfconsciously, almost impetuously, out of her thirst for the Divine. And there is something wholly in keeping with the Christian story that the first witness to the Resurrection—in a sense, one of the founders of the faith—should be an ex-prostitute. It's good to have something so subversive of spiritual priggishness smack dab at the center of the story.

But there's something else that links these women. There is a lavishness of emotion in all these stories. Mary Magdalene is an ambassador from a world very unlike the cold northern world where Christianity would establish its most powerful home; she is a creature of the Mediterranean, of the luxurious lands of the sun where people ate lying down. Imaginatively, at least, the love goddesses of the Mediterranean world are her cousins, with their sensual excesses transformed into excesses of love. At the wine miracle of Cana, Jesus gave a nod to old Bacchus across the wine-dark sea. In Mary Magdalene, the beauties of the scented and sensuous world of the East could be welcomed into the full picture of humanness that Christianity was painting.

The Feast of Mary Magdalene arrives in the middle of summer, and Mary Magdalene is an icon of relaxation. One of the great glimpses of her in the Gospels is of Mary at her ease with Jesus, next to him on the dirt floor in the cool of the little mud house in Bethany. She enjoys the presence of Christ. "She has chosen the better part," Jesus says in Luke to her bustling sister Martha. This is a pretty clear signal that what Mary is doing is somehow the essence of the Christian life. Martha is too busy to enjoy Christ. Mary likes to be near him, to sit quietly in the presence, "just relaxed and paying attention," as the Byrds sang. In Christian story and symbol, this is the state of humanity in Paradise —naturally, easily, happily in the presence of God.

Christian teaching is associated with the idea of a great and disastrous rupture with God, the original sin. One way to set it right, in some styles of thought, is repentance in sackcloth and ashes, turning away from all that is naturally human. This is perhaps the dominant strain in popular Christianity, particularly in the West.

But there's another strain, just as old and orthodox. This is the tradition out of which come mystics and contemplatives who hunger and thirst to experience the restored presence now. It comes from the Psalter ("My soul pants for God like the deer for the water brook, as in a dry and thirsty land") by way of John the Evangelist and the Patriarchs of Alexandria, kept alive in the Eastern Church, whose book of sacred instruction is called the *Philokalia* ("love of beauty"). In the West it comes through Julian of Norwich, Meister Eckhart, Thomas Traherne, George MacDonald, Evelyn Underhill, and many others, both famous and obscure. Their archetype in the Gospels is the woman at the well (one of the faces of

Mary Magdalene) who says, "Give me this living water!" Again and again they express their passion in images of hunger and thirst and even erotic desire. They witness to a natural desire for God that simply needs to be allowed to flow toward its beloved. Even stern Augustine says, "Our hearts were made for thee, and will never find rest nor peace 'til they rest in thee." Origen, one of the Egyptian Church fathers, talked about "Eros for God."

It is this way that Jesus seems to be calling the "better part" in the story of his visit to Mary and Martha. The point of spiritual practice is to restore Paradise, life lived consciously with God, to come back to the summer country. This is not a quick or easy process. For many people, it is a life's work, and even then is not complete. It hardly means a life without suffering either, but it is the goal of the Christian spiritual life. It makes sense that Mary, who chose the better part, is the first to experience the risen life in the garden outside the tomb. She has the thirst.

The gospel figure of Mary Magdalene is an icon of the role that desire plays in spiritual life. Eastern religious traditions—Hinduism and Buddhism in particular—teach that desire has to disappear. In the Western tradition, desire is central. We must want God with "all our heart, all our soul, and all our mind." Mary always wants to be near Jesus.

One of the names for the Promised Land in the Old Testament is *Beulah*, the "married land," the land that has joined with God like a woman with a man. Judeo-Christian spirituality has long spoken about the soul's relationship to God in images of marriage and erotic love. The greatest example of this is the Song of Solomon, or Song of Songs. I think it's fair to say that the Song of Songs is the most surprising book in the Bible. If you doubt me, put this book down right now, find a Bible, and read it. It will take about ten minutes, and you will finish it with a different idea of the Bible. And yes, all those images mean exactly what you think they mean.

The Song of Songs is surprising not for *what* it is—a great poem of erotic love, a lush Eastern lyric, a rhapsody on the spiritual and physical delights of love, probably an epithalamium, or celebratory wedding verse—but for *where* it is. How it got into the middle of the Hebrew Bible no one knows. It is traditionally said to be a story of the love of King Solomon and the dark maiden of the Shulamites. For millennia, rabbis, scholars, and Christian theologians have interpreted it symbolically as an allegory of the love of God for Israel or of Christ for the Church. While these readings can be illuminating, there's no disguising the poem's origin in human experience.

Mary Magdalene is associated with the Song of Songs, and the liturgy for her feast includes readings from it. It was apparently Hippolytus, bishop of Rome in the early third century, in his commentary on Song of Songs, who first made this connection. Just as it was a piece of wisdom to place this poem in the middle of the Bible, it was a piece of deep wisdom to associate Mary Magdalene with the beloved of the Song—Mary, carrying again her jar of perfumed oils, searching for her love by torchlight in the dark of Easter morning, like the Beloved of the Song. Bishop Hippolytus inserted into the heart of the Scriptures this most sensuous depiction of longing. It is an idea like the wafting of incense, a suggestion, a deepening of the imagination around the idea of a spiritual partner of Christ, a beloved bringing with her all the beauty and joy of the world. The catalog of pleasures of the heart and senses in the Song of Songs, of flowers and fruit, animals, bodies, landscape, adornment, comfort, ecstasy, this world so completely offered—this is Christ's beloved, the world that waits for him in the garden outside the tomb. It is the fulfilled and married land, the overflowing world of summer.

Redeemed, unfallen nature is the old earth goddesses with the demons driven out. She's like Isis of Egypt, who searches for the broken body of her beloved Osiris and restores him to life. Man and woman are together again in the new Easter garden as they were in the first garden. Full, whole nature, including human nature, does not lead away from God but toward God. Nature restored to eternity is nature with meaning and spirit.

Nervous Christians sometimes natter on about the dangers of "nature worship"—as if any human ever literally worshipped a rock or stream or mountain or tree. The very idea of nature that we express when we talk about nature worship would have been foreign to our ancestors. When we use the word *nature*, it carries a connotation born of eighteenth-century science, which saw nature as merely a mechanical system. But prehistoric humans were unable to conceive of nature as separate from spirit. They recognized and venerated the Divine that was present in mountain, forest, and meadow. "Nature worship" is a spiritual danger only when we define nature to exclude God.

Origen of Alexandria, writing about the solar system, said, "We do not wish to express contempt for these glorious works of God or to say . . . that sun, moon, and stars are nothing more than fiery lumps of matter . . . We are sure that Helios and Selene (Sun and Moon), through his only-begotten Son, offer their prayers to Almighty God." It seems to me that if Bishop Origen would not express contempt for the sun and moon as mere lumps of matter, he wouldn't express contempt for a tree, either. He might also see it as something capable of "offering prayer"—that is, possessing some kind of divinely given spirit—perhaps even consciousness.

So Magdalene's place in summer is poetically appropriate. She is an emblem of redeemed

ADAM WATCHING EVE SLEEP, BY GUSTAVE DORÉ, 1866. SUMMER IS A SACRAMENT OF
PARADISE RESTORED—MALE AND FEMALE, TOGETHER AGAIN IN THE GARDEN.

nature, of the holy enjoyment of the natural world, and the natural desire for God in the human heart. This natural desire is expressed in contemplative spirituality, of which she is a patroness. The point of contemplative practice is to learn to see God in what we're presented with, as Mary could see Christ in the gardener; to work long, slowly, and patiently to shed the barriers to fulfillment of our real desire. It is not the path of outer works, of ethics and engagement, but the path of longing for the companionship of God. It is what animates the various Marys of the Gospels and why they can be imaginatively combined into one figure.

The Year of the Lord is an epic work of sacramental art. Church tradition made the inspired choice to place Mary Magdalene's feast day at the height of summer, in the kingdom of ease where there is no more striving. We've been through the discipline of fall and winter; Advent and Lent have passed. Now at the height of summer we are all with Magdalene in the garden. In the free space created by Jesus' gaze, we have room, ease, and relaxation to step into our true nature.

Contemplatives, mystics, and poets live with a dim sense that Heaven lies just on the other side of a thin veil of perception, and they are troubled their whole lives by this apprehension. The story of the Magdalene says that love is all we need to see it clearly.

Mary Magdalene leads us along unexpected paths that run through the mass of scripture and theology like veins of silver in a wall of rock. She's not just a person who may have lived two thousand years ago, not even a memorable character in a great myth. Like everything else in the story of Christ, she is a living reality.

Some summer afternoon, when you are tired and hot from work or travel, or when you have spent your spirit on a meaningless day, and the world seems glaring and harsh, it may happen that something passes over you, cool and scented—a promise of water for your thirst, balm for your bruises, refreshment for your body, ripe fruit for your hunger, and wisdom for your heart—from the oldest and deepest well in the desert. Look for it in the breeze or the green leaves or the border of gold along the tops of the trees and the edges of the clouds. It is "Mariham the Happy" who consoles and anoints all flesh, who comes your way out of the shimmering distance.

## The Story

"After this he went journeying from town to town and village to village, proclaiming the good news of the Kingdom of God. With him were the Twelve and a number of women who had been set free from evil spirits and infirmities" (Luke 8:1–2). The Gospels make it clear that one of the sources of support for the Jesus movement is these women, "set free from evil spirits and infirmities," who "provided for them (the Twelve) out of their own resources." Among these is Mary Magdalene.

Her name tells us that she came from Magdala, a relatively large city on the western shore of the Sea of Galilee, known for its salt trade. A tradition, independent from the one that depicts her as a prostitute, says that she was wealthy, a businesswoman.

But there are a number of odd things in the passage from Luke. Adult men and women wayfaring together, not married to each other and not even related, must have been seen as peculiar, if not scandalous. Also, these women apparently have resources that they are free to dispose of as they choose. Are they widows? Businesswomen? Are they really living this vagabond life with Jesus and his male followers? Although there is emerging evidence that women played more of a role in early synagogue life than has been previously thought, the prominent place of women in the Jesus movement and later in the early churches in the Graeco-Roman world is striking.

The Gospels say that Jesus was accused of associating with "tax collectors and prostitutes." Even though this is said by enemies, it fits the spirit of his work. The gist of Jesus' ministry is that he pretty much associated with everybody. There are recurring stories in the Gospels where Jesus deals most gently with women involved in sexual immorality of one kind or another. There is the woman of "immoral life" whom we saw at the Pharisees' dinner anointing Jesus' feet; the Samaritan woman at the well, and the famous incident of the woman taken in adultery, who prompts the saying about the one without sin throwing the first stone. It seems as if there must have been a memory of Jesus' gentleness with women who had gotten themselves into sexual trouble (and that kind of trouble could be very bad, up to and including execution). Think of someone inserting himself between three or four Taliban soldiers with rifles and a kneeling woman in a *burqa*. That one of these women became a follower doesn't seem strange.

In fact, Jesus doesn't have much to do with *married* women aside from his mother. Among his most significant followers are that funny little family in Bethany, the two sisters, Mary and Martha, and their brother Lazarus—no parents, spouses, or children. There seems to be a profound reciprocal attachment among the four of them. (The death of Lazarus is the occasion for the famous two-word sentence in John, "Jesus wept"—the only time he does so in the Gospels.)

Pope Gregory the Great is the artist of Mary Magdalene, the one who made explicit the suggestion of a theme linking the various female bit players into a major role. It was he who, in sermons from the early seventh century, blended these gospel characters into the composite Mary Magdalene. Christian legend would later elaborate on her life. One story says that the wedding at Cana was the marriage of Mary Magdalene and St. John, the evangelist and beloved apostle. According to some traditions, Mary (like the Virgin Mary) died at Ephesus, the home of John's community, possibly as a martyr. A Provençal legend from the ninth century says that Mary, with her sister Martha and brother Lazarus, were cast adrift on the Mediterranean in a rudderless boat landing near Marseilles. Lazarus became the first bishop of the region, while Mary retired to a contemplative life in a cave where she was tended by angels and ascended to Heaven each day. Her remains are said to be at Vezelay, in Provence.

From what scholars have learned about the atmosphere and practice of the earliest Christian communities in the Middle East and in Europe, it seems possible that one of Jesus' original female followers could have founded and led a community as some of the other apostles did, or acted as a teacher or prophetess, or in some other role of spiritual leadership. A number of the apostles and early evangelists had schools that took on their names and authority after their deaths, and one can imagine there having been a school of Mary Magdalene. The fragmentary Gospel of Mary, which may date from the second century, pictures Mary Magdalene as the primary interpreter of Jesus' teachings to the apostles.

A woman's testimony was invalid in Jewish law at that time, so the striking fact that women, and Mary Magdalene in particular, are mentioned so prominently in the Gospels, and especially as witnesses to the Resurrection, is thought by some scholars to be powerful evidence in favor of the historical truth of their role in Jesus' mission.

In the first centuries of the Church, there was another tradition of Mary Magdalene that has become clear only in recent decades. In some early Christian communities she was an even more important figure than she seems in the Gospels. There is a small library of early Christian documents—some of them called gospels, some of them arguably as old in their origins as the four canonical gospels—that portrays a body of beliefs, stories, and teachings that did not get into the New Testament. A trove of them was discovered in 1945 buried in a jar at Nag Hammadi in rural Upper Egypt near the site of one of the first Christian monasteries. The Church, understandably, has not figured out what to do with them, but they are, like it or not, technically new gospels—that grail of biblical scholarship—and they contain previously unknown teachings that claim to come from Jesus Christ. Parts of them closely parallel the New Testament; much is wildly different. Some of the content may be reconcilable with orthodox theology and spirituality; some is probably not. Much of the material is obscure and confusing, apparently referring to mystical teachings, rites, and practices that are not explained in the text. Scholarly research into these documents and gospels is in its infancy.

Theologically, they are what is broadly called "gnostic." *Gnosis* means "knowledge" in Greek. Gnosticism is not a religion, but an approach to religion that seeks a knowledge or experience of God that saves or redeems in this life. Gnosticism pictures the body and the material world as illusions in which the soul is trapped. However, the soul can recall its true home in the celestial realms and eventually return to it. This recollection is the saving knowledge or gnosis.

This is obviously different from Judeo-Christian teaching about the goodness and reality of our world and its divine creation. Yet certain orthodox authorities—early fathers, arguably St. Paul himself—seem to say that there is a Christian gnosis, a transformative direct knowledge of God, and a system of belief and practice to obtain it. There were gnostic varieties of Christianity for centuries after Jesus' death, many of them quite popular. Orthodoxy proved stronger in the end. Gnostic Christianity became one of the minor exotica of history until the discovery of the Nag Hammadi documents.

Some of these Gnostic Christian documents—The Dialogue of the Savior, the Pistis Sophia, the Gospel of Mary Magdalene, the Gospel of Philip—show an extraordinary body of early belief centered on Mary Magdalene that expands on her cryptic role in the orthodox Gospels. In this tradition she is, after Christ, the most important figure in the movement. She is "Magdalene, the one who is called his [Jesus'] companion"; "The happy one, beautiful in her speaking"; "the woman who knew the All"; "the one who is the inheritor of the light"; "the Apostle who excels the rest." These works show Mary Magdalene as Jesus' special and closest companion, the one with the gift of understanding the deepest implications of his teaching, who interprets it to the more earthy male disciples. She even becomes a cosmic character, the *Sophia* (the Greek translation of the Hebrew word for the wisdom of God). She is the divine wisdom which has become lost or fallen and is restored to her rightful place by Christ. Did this belief in the Magdalene's status grow from the few hints in the canonical Gospels, or did a tradition of the extraordinary position and authority of Mary Magdalene come first, to be later modified in the four Gospels?

Contemplation is the branch of Christian spirituality that works with a person's desire for the felt presence of God in their life. In his *Introduction to the Devout Life*, from the early seventeenth century, St. Francis de Sales refers to contemplation as *"le vray exercice de Magdelaine"*—the true exercise of the Magdalene. Mt. Athos in Greece is the home of some twenty Greek Orthodox monasteries dedicated to the contemplative life, and Mary Magdalene is the patroness of the whole settlement. The original connection of Mary Magdalene with the contemplative life comes from the story of Jesus' visit to the home of Mary and Martha as told in the Gospel of Luke. Martha is busy cooking and caring for the guests; Mary sits and listens to Jesus. The sisters were taken by the Church as symbols of the two Christian spiritual types, active and contemplative.

The approach that Mary Magdalene symbolizes is similar to the teaching of the Sufis, the mystical branch of Islam. Many people today are attracted to Sufi thought through the writings of Rumi, a thirteenth-century Sufi poet. In Rumi's poetry, as elsewhere in Sufi spirituality, God is spoken of as "the Beloved," analogous to an earthly beloved, who is sought with all the passion of one's heart. Hippolytus uses the image of Mary Magdalene going to the tomb in the dark of Easter morning with her anointing oil and spices in a way that recalls the Sufi symbolism of the lover passionately seeking the Divine.

The Mary Magdalene experience, the experience of the presence of God, is the first source of any genuine spiritual teaching. When the experience becomes too rare or distant, when the message is too many messengers removed from the Magdalene, it's time to be wary. Mary of Magdala, she who had taken leave of her senses, is the first to come fully to her senses, to have the doors of her perception cleansed. She turns away from the tomb, toward the Gardener.

## *Entering the Season*

**Contemplative Prayer**—Today there are many resources for those interested in developing a Christian spiritual practice. The best place I know to begin is Father Thomas Keating's *Open Mind, Open Heart*. It is available through most bookstores or may be ordered through Keating's organization, Contemplative Outreach, which offers resources for developing a contemplative practice. They may be contacted via their website at <www.centeringprayer.com/> or by mail at Contemplative Outreach Ltd., P.O. Box 737, 10 Park Place, Suite 2B, Butler, NJ 07405 (973-838-3384).

**Goddesses**—Spend some time with the way female divinity was expressed in ancient cultures. Look especially at the four famously graceful golden goddesses who guard Pharaoh Tutankhamun's canopic shrine. Selket, goddess of magic and healing; Nut, the embracing sky; Nephthys, protector of the dead; and Isis, the great queen and mother. Like Mary Magdalene, these women wait and watch at the tomb.

**Weddings**—Summer is when earth and sky find each other again, the married season, as Israel in the Old Testament is the married land. Not for nothing does the idea of June brides still linger. Marriage is the spiritual symbol of fulfillment, fruition, harmony, and wholeness. Wedding traditions in other cultures suggest even more strongly the ritual content of this sacrament of male and female. Reflect on your own wedding, your parents', your daughter's. Look at relics from the wedding—old wedding dresses, photo albums, videos. There is a strange and poignant solemnity that intrudes into even the most ordinary wedding.

## MUSIC

Tapestry, *Song of Songs: Come Into My Garden—A Portrait of Sensual and Spiritual Love* (Telarc CD-80486, 1998).

*Umm Kulthum, A Voice Like Egypt,* narrated by Omar Sharif (video).

Fairouz, *Very Best* – Vol. 1.

Ofra Haza, *Yemenite Songs* (Globe Style-City Hall) and *Desert Wind* (Wea/Warner Bros).

Natacha Atlas *Halim* (Beggars Banquet CD).

## READING

Ariel Bloch and Chana Bloch, *The Song of Songs: A New Translation with an Introduction and Commentary* (University of California Press, 1998).

A GOLDEN HARVEST, BY GEORGE TURNER (1843-1910). *THE MARRIED LAND;*
*NATURE FULFILLED: "THE EARTH, AND EVERY COMMON SIGHT . . .*
*APPARELL'D IN CELESTIAL LIGHT . . ."*

# 13

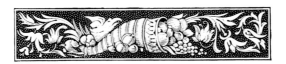

# AUGUST 6

## THE FEAST OF THE TRANSFIGURATION

*When the doors of perception are cleansed,*
*then we would see everything as it is—infinite.*

—William Blake

*Mercifully grant that we,*
*being delivered from the disquietude of this world,*
*may by faith behold the King in his beauty.*

—Prayer for the Feast of the
Transfiguration

*The Corn was Orient and Immortal Wheat which never should be reaped, nor*
*was ever sown. I thought it had stood from Everlasting to Everlasting. The Dust*
*and the Stones of the Street were as precious as Gold. . . . Boys and girls tum-*
*bling in the street and playing were moving jewels. I knew not that they were*
*born or should die. . . . Eternity was manifest in the light of day, and something*
*infinite behind everything appeared.*

—Thomas Traherne, *Centuries*
*of Meditation*

*There was a time when meadow, grove, and stream,*
*The earth, and every common sight,*
*To me did seem*
*Apparell'd in celestial light.*

—William Wordsworth,
"Ode: Intimations of Immortality from
Recollections of Early Childhood"

## The Experience

We come to the end of our journey now, the last of the summer days of Jesus' company of friends wandering through the summer lands of the Galilee, the last high moment before autumn. The Year of the Lord has worked to clear our sight and deepen our spiritual senses. The summer's idyll brings us to a mountaintop, where we can see everything and look back and say good-bye. The journey starts again from here, but this time we're higher than before.

Most people are familiar with the sermon Martin Luther King delivered shortly before he was assassinated, in which he seemed to foresee his death. He used the Old Testament story about how Moses was allowed by God to see the Promised Land from Mt. Nebo, but forbidden to cross the Jordan and enter. "I've been to the mountaintop," King said. He'd seen the Promised Land, but, he cautioned, "I may not get there with you."

I wonder if he might not also have been thinking about the story of the Transfiguration, when Jesus goes to the mountaintop. On the summit of Mt. Tabor he is at the height of his glory, radiant with white light. When he comes down, he tells his friends about what will happen next. Abraham Lincoln was also assassinated at the height of his triumph, just as the Civil War ended. He too had strong presentiments of his death.

There is a pattern here that has to do with completion. With some people, there comes a sense that they have done all they can or came to do; they're finished. They have gone away from us already, even while they're still alive. Death reaches into life and establishes a perimeter around the person. The disciples must have sensed this about Jesus as soon as they experienced Transfiguration. "We'll build shelters for you," says Peter, the ever-lovably dense, as he witnesses this strange event. But the boundary around Jesus is already in place.

In the early days—May, June, July—it seems as if summer could last forever, as if it could abolish time at the top of a summer afternoon. By August, though, we know what's going to happen. We wanted this moment of ripe fullness, but it is filled with poignancy.

At this point in the Gospels (it seems to happen almost as soon as they start descending the mountain), Jesus begins to talk about his death. A very different path is ahead. Once you're at the top, all roads lead downward. That's the way it goes. Now we have to turn away from the sun and begin to enter the darkness.

August is summer that has heard a rumor of fall. It doesn't sparkle with the liveliness, motion, and lightness of May or June or the high, festive brightness of July. It shimmers away toward the horizon in a hot blue haze. I know a painter who says she sees a distinct kind of light in August, different from both summer and fall. The name of the month comes from the emperor Caesar Augustus, and the purple robes of those august caesars color the last of summer. Blue shadows hide in the corners, like the patches of cobalt light after a flashbulb goes off. A stillness falls, like one of those lapses in conversation around a dinner table. We're aware only in the vaguest way, but summer is already looking ahead to its end. Jesus takes his friends up Mt. Tabor to see everything. Here at the end of summer, the world shows us everything, caught in the still center of August.

Paul refers to Jesus as "the first fruits of those that sleep." In various times and places, the first days of August celebrated the first fruits of the coming harvest. In Ireland they observed *Lughnasadh* in honor of the great god Lugh. The first sheaf of wheat from the grain harvest was brought in procession to the top of a green hill and buried.

As Peter's talk of shelters suggests, the gospel account of the Transfiguration seems to have something to do with the ancient Jewish holiday of Succoth, the Feast of Tabernacles, or "booths," a festival of the harvest. In the Vatican, at mass on the Feast of the Transfiguration, the Pope crushes ripe grapes into the chalice. The Orthodox priests bless the orchards; people bring baskets of fruit to church. Heavy fruit hanging from tree and vine, full and rounded, glowing, its perfection accomplished, is a sacrament of the Transfiguration.

In the East, the feast in some places is called *Vartavarh*, or "rose flame," since, as early Armenian church chronicles explain, "Christ opened His glory like a rose on Mt. Tabor." The Transfiguration is the full flowering of Jesus' earthly life. Vartavarh, the rose flame of life opens up to let us see inside. The grapes are crushed, the rose flame glows through the red wine. This is the moment when everything is clear. Jesus on Mt. Tabor showed his friends

THE TRANSFIGURATION, BY FRA ANGELICO, 1442. THE RADIANCE AT THE SUMMIT OF THE YEAR: "ETERNITY WAS MANIFEST IN THE LIGHT OF DAY. . . ."

nothing more than what was already there. It was the apostles' eyes that changed, not Jesus. The doors of their perception, as William Blake says, were cleansed.

The United States dropped the atomic bomb on the city of Hiroshima on the Feast of the Transfiguration. It was hideously appropriate. Hiroshima was a satanic parody of the Transfiguration. Hiroshima is about breaking creation open to get at the hidden power, to compel human ends. The lesson of the Transfiguration is that the power inside creation is fully revealed to the prayerful and humble—the child that Peter plays on the mountain.

We've talked a lot about sacred time, but it's not only special times that offer an opening to the spirit—places can, too. The setting of the Transfiguration is a mountaintop. In religious symbolism around the world, mountaintops are where earth comes closest to Heaven, where time touches eternity. When you go to a mountain, you put yourself into a symbolic landscape. It's a place where the physically real is so close to the imaginatively or spiritually real that the usual distinction between these things tends to be less important.

A friend told me about his visit to the Lake District in the north of England with his wife, shortly after they were married. They had hiked and driven for a couple of days, and a sense had been growing as he looked around that this was in some way all he had ever wanted. On their third day in the mountains, they drove up a steep winding pass to view the ruins of a Roman fort. Near the top of the pass, they got out of the car to walk up the hillside. There was a tumbling stream that ran down to the road and an old stone to mark where three counties meet. He was a few yards ahead of his wife when in an instant, as he describes it, all of his self went away. All that was left was the world he was in: the cry of birds, the splash of the stream, the wind whistling through the hills, the ragged gray clouds, and the thick sheep-cropped grass of a hillside broken by gray stones. It wasn't that he felt a bond with the landscape. He, as he had always known himself, seemed to *be* those other things. There was no difference between sensing them and being them. The experience lasted maybe ten seconds. His wife called him to look at something and he came back. But his awareness, while it lasted, was utterly changed.

The prayer for the Transfiguration says, "Mercifully grant that we, being delivered from the disquietude of this world, may by faith behold the King in his beauty." The mental and emotional static that ordinarily passes for selfhood stopped for my friend. He was delivered from the disquietude of this world.

Walk down a country road in August. The land is golden-lazy. The year lies before us at the precise moment that everything is ripe but not yet harvested. As in the kind of timeless vision that Thomas Traherne describes, look at the flowers, grass, fruit, or crops as they are this moment—perfect. As Hamlet says, the ripeness is all. St. Paul calls the fulfillment of God's plan for creation the *pleroma* or fullness. August acts out the pleroma. In summer all bushes are the bush that burned and was not consumed.

When the sun is the highest, its power is most felt in the world, dwelling among us. Signs of the sun are everywhere—in the still ponds rimmed with tall grasses and green algae, the brown water at the center shining like a bronze mirror. The playfulness of spring and early summer has transformed into golden solemnity, a summer version of the pattern that descended at Advent. The sun hammers gold leaf over everything.

The white sunlight, the green fire of the foliage, the bronze light on the water, the luminous cobalt sky: All are caught in this moment, the end of summer, fixed in a thousand mosaic fragments, like a Persian miniature with the light flaring out.

*"And the fire that breaks from thee then, a billion times told lovelier, more dangerous."*

The fire that came down at Pentecost has filled the world and, from the world, is released to our senses. Like the apostles, the pilgrims of the year have this flame to carry into the dark. We shield our eyes, and say farewell.

## *The Story*

The Arabs call it *Jebel et Tur*, the "mountain of mountains." Nearly isolated on all sides and almost hemispherical in shape, Mt. Tabor, the Mount of the Transfiguration, rises suddenly from the flat Plain of Esdraelon (about five miles southeast of Nazareth) to a peak of 1,650 feet. The summit forms an oblong plateau about 1,000 feet wide and 3,000 feet long.

Tabor has always been a holy mountain. Because of its striking shape and site, it is frequently used as a metaphor or poetic image in the Hebrew Bible. In Canaanite culture, prominent peaks often had their own divine patrons and took their names from them. Scholars believe there was a *baal* or god of Tabor. *Tibira* or *tabura*, in the language of ancient Sumer, meant "blacksmith." This was one of the numerous personae of Tammuz, the god of fertility, also seen as the inventor of the art of metalworking. (The Tubal of Genesis 4:22, "the father of all coppersmiths and blacksmiths," may be this god.) Tammuz was one of the dying and rising gods of the ancient Near East. Mt. Tabor may have been one of the "groves and high places" condemned by the Israelite prophets. Recent excavation indicates the existence of a Hellenic temple on the mountain.

MT. TABOR, THE MOUNT OF THE TRANSFIGURATION,
IN THE GALILEE; HIGH SUMMER.

The mountain plays a role in Old Testament story as well as in Canaanite myth. Tabor is one of the traditional sites of the mysterious incident in Genesis when the priest-king Melchizedek blesses Abraham with bread and wine, symbolic predecessors of the Eucharist. Later, when the Promised Land is divided among the children of Jacob, Tabor marks the boundary between the lands of Issachar and Zebulon. In the Book of Judges, the prophetess Deborah secretly assembles the thousand Israelites on Tabor, who sweep down on the army of Sisera below. The Galilean city Daboura (now the village of Dab°riyéh) at the foot of the mountain commanded roads along which armies and caravans passed and so was among the Galilean cities taken by the empire-building pharaoh Rameses II. During the Jewish revolt against Rome in 70 C.E., Jewish rebels, pursued by the Roman army, took refuge there to organize a last stand. Led by the historian Josephus (later to jump ship to the Roman side) they circled the summit with two miles of earthworks. The Roman commander Placidus lured them by a ruse down to the plain and destroyed them.

The belief in Tabor as the scene of Christ's Transfiguration is first recorded in the fourth century, and no doubt began earlier. The mountain became a place of pilgrimage. A basilica and several churches and chapels were built on the summit. In 1101, Benedictine monks built a fortified abbey that withstood several Saracen attacks. After the critical Crusader defeat by Saladin at the Horns of Hattin in 1187, the monks fled the mountain. Today the plateau of Tabor is once again occupied by monks, Franciscan and Greek Orthodox.

The major Jewish feast of Succoth was a celebration of the harvest. It was held somewhat later (September or October) than the Feast of the Transfiguration, but there is a suggestion in the Gospels that the Transfiguration is connected to Succoth—or at least that it's supposed to remind us of Succoth, via Peter's suggestion that they build "booths" to shelter Jesus, Moses, and Elijah. Certainly the Transfiguration has connections to festivals of the early harvest.

The Feast of the Transfiguration, according to early Armenian church records, had its origin in an early harvest festival celebrated in the western highlands of Asia (Persia, Iran, maybe Afghanistan) dedicated to a goddess called Vartavarh, or Roseflame (early chroniclers identified her with Aphrodite, the Greek goddess of love). In the fourth century, St. Gregory the Illuminator adapted it for the Church as the Feast of the Transfiguration. The Christians kept the old name of the feast because, as the Armenian history says, "Christ opened his glory like a rose on Mt. Tabor."

In the East, the Feast of the Transfiguration has been celebrated continuously since that time. It is one of the twelve great festivals of the Orthodox calendar. In the Syriac Church it is a feast of the first class. In Armenian orthodoxy, it is preceded by a fast of six days and celebrated for three. In the West, the Feast of the Transfiguration is not mentioned before 850, and for centuries was observed only by certain monastic orders. It was not until 1457 that Pope Callistus III ordered its general observance. At the time of the Protestant Reformation, it was still felt in some countries to be a recent innovation, and so was not at first incorporated into many Reformation calendars.

The Celtic festival of Lughnasadh (also called "the earth's sorrowing in autumn") celebrated the early grain harvest at the beginning of August, and lasted from prehistory into the nineteenth century in much of Ireland, the Isle of Man, and south Wales. The Anglo-Saxons in England enjoyed a feast that may be related to Lughnasadh called the "loaf-mass," or "Lammas," because the first grain of the harvest was baked into loaves on that day. Many places in Scotland had Lammas fairs, some of which still survive. Archbishop Theodore ordained that the synods of the newly established church in England should be celebrated on Lammas. It remained an important day for official business throughout the Middle Ages. Interestingly, August 6, the day of the Transfiguration, was sometimes called "Old Lammas."

As we've seen, the four seasons were reckoned both by a solar calendar and an agricultural lunar calendar. In the solar calendar, the start of autumn is the equinox—Michaelmas. But in the old agricultural system, it is the opening of August that would have marked the start of autumn, the beginning of the fall.

## Entering the Season

**Fruit**—In late summer, many farms offer opportunities for families to pick summer fruits. You and your children can do as they do in Eastern Europe, where children and families select summer fruit and prepare baskets to give to their neighbors. If you own fruit trees or an orchard, this is a good time to have them blessed.

**The high old times**—Remember a time in your life that you tend to think of as "the good old days," a period when things came together and worked for a while in a way that seemed right. Maybe it was a job where the work and the coworkers meshed, a project you shared with other people, a neighborhood you lived in, a school, a period in your family's life. As you recall it, see if you can see a pattern in why it worked, if there was a climax or high point, and how it eventually disbanded and went back to ordinary life. All good things must end, and we have to accept the dissolution of the circle. How can you incorporate the ending of that good thing into the larger pattern of life?

**Peak moments**—These moments of more intense life may develop out of high excitement; spiritual practice; the growth of a relationship; travel; strong aesthetic experiences with music, art, or literature; or the flash of a great idea. But even in very ordinary times, there are instants that stand out—insights, moments when things become clear and fall into place. It is in the nature of these moments to be fleeting, and the more we try to hold onto them or recreate them, the further away they go. But do they call us to something? Is there a way to take them back down the mountainside?

**The harvest**—If you know any family farmers, August is a good time to visit. There's an epochal farm crisis going on right now, and we will all lose if the family-farm system goes under. Read about family-farm issues and write to your congressional representatives to support farmer-friendly initiatives. If there are farms near your community, join a community-supported agriculture group that buys produce directly from those farmers.

## READING

William Wordsworth, "Ode: Intimations of Immortality from Recollections of Early Childhood"; "Lines Composed a Few Miles Above Tintern Abbey;" etc. Wordsworth gave us a vocabulary for talking about spirit in nature.

T. S. Eliot, *The Four Quartets.* "Humankind cannot bear very much reality," the man said, and here the greatest poet in the English language of the twentieth century, at the far reach of his powers, conveys as much reality as he can in this quiet, strange, and bottomlessly evocative group of mystical poems. Especially relevant in the context of the Transfiguration is "Burnt Norton," a summer vision on a hot afternoon, as a dry old garden becomes Heaven for a moment.

# LIST OF ILLUSTRATIONS AND CREDITS

*The author and publisher wish to thank those who have kindly given permission to reproduce the illustrations found in this book.*

Page xiv: *Diagram of the Four Seasons,* folio 57R of Breviary of Love, 13th century Provencal codex by Ermengol de Béziers. The Art Archive/Real Biblioteca de lo Escorial/Dagli Orti.

Page 3: Winslow Homer (1836-1910), *Snap the Whip,* 1872. Oil on canvas, 22" x 36". Collection of The Butler Institute of American Art, Youngstown, Ohio.

Page 16: St. Catherine's Monastery, Sinai. Collection of the author.

Page 19: Tomb of Second Temple Period, Jerusalem. Richard T. Nowitz/CORBIS.

Page 21: Detail of Sun Mosaic in San Paolo Maggiore, 1641 by Dionisio Lazzari and Valentini e Tacca, 1641. Mimmo Jodice/CORBIS.

Page 27: Christ as sun god Apollo. Early Christian mosaic. Mid-third century. Grotte, St. Peter's Basilica, Vatican State. Scala/Art Resource, NY

Page 32: Raphael (1483-1520), *Saint Michael.* Réunion des Musées Nationaux/ Art Resource, NY.

Page 35: Joseph Mallord William Turner (1775-1851), *The Angel Standing in the Sun.* The Art Archive/ Tate Gallery London/Eileen Tweedy.

Page 38: Maurice Sand, *La Chasse a Baudet.* Illustration for George Sand's *Legendes Rustiques.* Mary Evans Picture Library.

Page 41: Glastonbury Tor. Colin Hoskins; Cordaiy Photo Library Ltd./CORBIS

Page 44: W. Small, illustration from Harper's Monthly, 1890. Mary Evans Picture Library.

Page 49: Albrecht Dürer (1471-1528), *Jesus Born.* Mary Evans Picture Library.

Page 60: William Morris Hunt (1824-79), *Stag in the Moonlight,* ca. 1857. Smithsonian American Art Musuem, Museum purchase.

Page 73: *Young Christmas Carolers.* Hulton Deutsch Collection/CORBIS.

Page 76: *The Nativity,* Russian School, 16th century tempera on panel. Private Collection/Bridgeman Art Library.

Page 82: *Children Seated at Fireplace.* Underwood & Underwood/CORBIS.

# INDEX

QUEST BOOKS
are published by
The Theosophical Society in America
Wheaton, Illinois 60189-0270,
a worldwide, nonprofit membership organization
that promotes fellowship among all peoples of the world,
encourages the study of religion, philosophy, and science,
and supports spiritual growth and healing.

Today humanity is on the verge of becoming, for the first time in its history, a global community. The only question is what kind of community it will be. Quest Books strives to fulfill the purpose of the Theosophical Society to act as a leavening; to introduce into humanity a large mindedness, a freedom from bias, an understanding of the values of the East and West; and to point the way to human development as a means of service, both for the individual and for the whole of humankind.

For more information about Quest Books,
visit **www.questbooks.net**
For more information about the Theosophical Society,
visit **www.theosophical.org**,
or contact **Olcott@theosmail.net**,
or (630) 668-1571.

*The Theosophical Publishing House is aided by*
*the generous support of the Kern Foundation,*
*a trust dedicated to Theosophical education.*